PLIGHT OF THE MINORITIES

PLIGHT OF THE MINORITIES:
Problems and Grievances in their Education

R.N. THAKUR

GYAN PUBLISHING HOUSE
NEW DELHI-110002

PLIGHT OF THE MINORITIES:
Problems and Grievances in their Education
[*Education, Sociology*]

ISBN: 81-212-0624-3

Published in 1999 in India by
Gyan Publishing House
5, Ansari Road
New Delhi 110 002

Laser Typeset at Alphabet, Delhi
Printed at Mehra Offset Press, New Delhi.

Contents

Preface

In all developing nations problems and grievances of the minorities' education remained a hitherto neglected area.

Any study relating to any management of the educational institutions, their grievances, etc., is directly concerned with human beings; and, hence, poses an ethical dilemma. Ethical issues are posed by the potential consequences of the publication, or, utilization of the research findings.

The subjects of this study, the minority managed educational institutions' management, heads of institutions, teaching and non-teaching staff, the parents, might sometimes find its results offensive, either because they are portrayed in a light they find unappealing, or because attitudes and modes of behaviour, they would prefer to keep private are made public. In several settings of social life some people engage in practices which they do not want to become public. For instance, some people in the institutions, mismanage, maladminister, do not pay full salary, etc. Would they like that these should become public knowledge?

It is the obligation of any social research to collect and organise facts and make findings public.

To make findings public is one of the main contributions social research can make to the fostering of a 'free and open society'.

'A good study might make somebody angry'.

If a research study is done competently and the conclusions drawn are backed by facts and good arguments, there is nothing to fear or be angry.

It is to be kept in view that the overriding obligation of every social research is to promote 'free and open discussion of social issues'.

It is for the readers to judge how far and in what perspective the social issues have been placed before them.

One is simply amazed to note that the grievances of the minority managed educational institutions are numerous, many of these are also the common grievances of other non-minority institutions, yet there was relative lack of concern for a systematic study of these problems so as to make any modest attempt to remedy the situation and to make the educational condition any better.

The condition of education among the Buddhists and the Muslims is deplorable. The Christians, the Parsis, the Sikhs are much better as compared to the Buddhists and the Muslims.

The state of professional, technical, vocational education; and education among women, particularly among Muslims, is disappointing.

In the name of educational rights of the minorities, in some regions, a deceptive situation has been created. The real interest of education of the backward among these minorities, greatly suffers. No doubt, the contributions of numerous organizations are like silver linings in the dark clouds. Their efforts are noteworthy and deserve encouragement. The following lines from the correspondence of a respondent from a Parsi organization give us a view of the situation, and a hope they cherish:

> I am sure your research on above subject will prove very useful to the minority communities as looking to the index of cost of living going up and up every month it is becoming impossible for minority communities to run educational institutions to balance their budget; and it would be in the fitness of circumstances that these institutions be provided with sufficient funds as these schools conducted by minority communities are not given grants by the government and you will doubtless appreciate that teachers should be paid lucrative salaries by way of remuneration, etc., so that they could work with dedication and zeal.

F.J. Antia,
R.D. Sethna Scholarship Fund, Bombay

This sums up the crux of the problem which generally besets the minority managed educational institutions in almost all parts of the country.

This study makes an attempt to pinpoint the grievances of

the minority managed educational institutions among five designated religious minority communities, viz., the Buddhists, the Christians, the Muslims, the Parsis, and the Sikhs.

Part One of the book relates to the conceptual and constitutional aspects of the minorities. Part Two is devoted to the study of the financial grievances of the minority managed educational institutions covering fifteen major States and Union Territories. Part Three is devoted to the study of the non-financial and sundry other grievances of these institutions. In parts two and three, grievances are also separately documented state-wise. Some financial and non-financial grievances also overlap.

If the outcome and recommendations, based on hard facts of the situation, as incorporated in the book have any policy implication and administrative backup, the investment of talents, time and resources may be considered as amply rewarded. Even otherwise, the author shall have the satisfaction of doing a piece of work which was really needed.

Between what the people want and what they need; what the governments want and do and what the people need, if there is any harmony achieved in the area of removal of the grievances of the minority managed educational institutions leading to the educational development among them, through the good offices of the governments, and various other agencies efforts in this study will be deemed to be amply rewarded.

Delhi
25th December 1998

R.N. Thakur

[illegible] the Christians, the Muslims, the Parsis and the Sikhs.

[illegible]

[illegible]

[illegible]

R.N. [illegible]

Acknowledgements

First of all, we owe our thanks to the various government authorities both in the Centre and States, who supported this study and gave an opportunity to go into the problems and grievances of the minority managed educational institutions in India. Various non-governmental organizations and other institutions from which the support flowed also deserve mention.

Notable among these are:

Abul Kalam Azad Education Society, Yadgiri.
Al-Ameen Progressive Educational Society, Belgaum.
Al-Ansar Welfare and Educational Society, Malegaon.
Al-Azmat Educational Society, Hyderabad.
Al-Hasnat Socio-Educational Society, Hyderabad.
Al-Hira Educational and Welfare Society, Aurangabad.
Al-Huda Education Society, Bidar.
Al-Kabir Education Society, Mysore.
As-Suffa Education Trust, Bellary.
Associations of Urdu Education Societies, Aurangabad.
Bhartiya Bauddha Shiksha Parishad, Lucknow.
Bidar District Muslim Welfare Association, Bidar.
Catholic Bishop's Conference of India Centre, New Delhi.
Chandigarh Administration, Chandigarh.
Church of North India, Nagpur.
Deeni Taleemi Council, Lucknow.
Delhi Sikh Gurudwara Management Committee, New Delhi.
Directorate of Public Instruction, Thiruvananthapuram.
Directorate of Public Instruction, Punjab.
Department of Education, Government of Rajasthan.
Dr Baba Saheb Ambedkar Smarak Samiti, Deeksha Bhoomi, Nagpur.

Dandeli Education Society, Dandeli.
Department of Education, Government of Gujarat.
Fateh Educational Society, Hubli.
Friday Club, Chalakudy.
General Department of Education, Government of Kerala.
Ghalib Education Society, Bangalore.
Hamdard Education Society, New Delhi.
Hilal Education Society, Mysore.
Ideal Mahila Mandal, Gulbarga.
Islamic Information Centre, New Delhi.
Islamic Research and Analysis Centre, West Bengal.
Jammate-E-Islami Hind, Calicut, Kerala.
Joint Editor, Educational Monthly, Malegaon.
Karnataka Rajya Urdu Teachers' Association, Bangalore.
Karnataka State Minorities Commission, Bangalore.
Khaja Education Society, Gulbarga.
Khalsa Medical and Education Trust, Bangalore.
Khatibi Service Society, Bangalore.
Mahabodhi Society, Sarnath, Varanasi.
Madari Education Society, Tumkur.
Madina Educational Society, Hyderabad.
Madresa Arabia Qasimul Uloom Chharra, Aligarh.
Minorities Educational and Welfare Trust, Jaipur.
Minorities Commission, Government of India.
Millat Educational Society, Dhanbad.
Muslim Educational Society, Calicut, Kerala.
Muslim Association, Thiruvananthapuram.
Mysore Educational Social and Cultural Organisation, Mysore.
New Muslim Educational Society, Saharanpur.
National Education Trust, Ankola.
Office of Parsi Panchayat, Bombay.
Organisation of Muslim Educational Institutions and Associations of Tamil Nadu, Madras.
Peoples' Education Society, Bombay.
Roshni Education Society, Pune.
State Minorities Commission, Patna.
St. Thomas Aquinas Educational Society, Bangalore.

St. Anthony's Educational Society, Honavar.
State Minorities Commission, Madras, Tamil Nadu.
Students' Islamic Organisation, Manipur.
The Minorities Educational Institutions Association, Lucknow, UP.
U.S.W. Shirgaokar Educational Trust, Ugarkhurd.
Uttar Pradesh Basic Shiksha Parishad, Allahabad.
Vocational Education Society, Gulbarga.
V.M.E. Society, Vaniyambadi, Tamil Nadu.
Xavier Educational Trust, Mangalore.

No less than the organisations there are numerous individuals whose constant help and inspiration went into the making of this comprehensive study. Our thanks are due to them.

Notable among the individuals who continued to assist in this important work are:

Arnavaz Mama, Managing Editor, Parsiana, Bombay.
M. Zahid Khan, President of Students' Islamic Organisation, Manipur Zone.
A. Abdussalam, Pro-Vice-Chancellor, Mahatma Gandhi University, Kottayam.
Father Joseph, General Secretary, All India Association of Catholic Educational Institutions, CBCI Centre, Delhi.
F.J. Antia, R.D. Sethna Scholarship Fund, Bombay.
G.J. Tata, Joint Secretary, Office of Trustees of Parsi Panchayat Funds and Properties, Bombay.
H.M. Khan, Minorities Education and Welfare Trust, Jaipur.
K.M. Arifuddin, Secretary, Madina Education Centre, Hyderabad.
M. Riazuddin Ahmad, General Secretary, Minorities Educational Institutions Association, Lucknow.
M.A. Mateen, Secretary, Andhra Pradesh, Minorities Commission, Hyderabad.
Mir Kamaluddin Ali Khan, Research Scholar, Osmania University.
M.H. Gazali, Institute of Objective Study, Jamia Nagar, New Delhi.
M.I. Deshmukh, Retired Superintendent of Education, Buldana.

Mohsin Kamal, President, Bidar District Muslim Welfare Association.

Mohammad Ashfaque Ahmad, Jamaate-E-Islami Hind, New Delhi.

Mary Parmar, Shimla.

Md. Iqbal Ahmad, Coordinator, Society for Friendship, Education and Development, New Delhi.

Rivatha Banth, Sarnath.

Saiyid Hamid, Hamdard Education Society, New Delhi.

Sharafat H. Khan, General Secretary, Rajasthan Educational and Scientific Society, Jaipur.

S.M. Iqbal, Head of the Department of Urdu, Bhagalpur University.

S. Rajinder Singh Monga, President, Delhi Sikh Management Committee, New Delhi.

S.N.H. Razvi, Secretary, Karnataka State Minorities Commission, Bangalore.

T.K. Damodaran, Principal, Dr. Ambedkar College, Nagpur.

Ven. Dharampal Mahathe, Bengal Buddhist Temple, Calcutta.

Ven. L. Ariyawansa Nayaka MahaThero, Vice-President, Maha Buddhist Society, New Delhi.

Ven. Maha Guru Narbu Lama, Assam Buddha Dham, Lakhanpani, Assam.

Z.S. Saiyed, Chairman 15-point Programme, Bharuch, Gujarat.

We are particularly thankful to Shri Saiyid Hamid for his kindness in making available to us a copy of the survey report of Muslim managed educational institutions, conducted by Hamdard Education Society over a decade ago, and published by them in 1982-83. We are equally beholden to Shri Mohammad Ashfaque Ahmad, Secretary (Education), Jamaate-E-Islami Hind, New Delhi, and Shri M.A. Gazali, Director, Institute of Objective Study, New Delhi, for their continued support and suggestions. Shri H.U. Azmi, Superintendent, Deeni Taleemi Council, Uttar Pradesh, deserves no less praise for keeping us abreast of the core of the problems faced by the Muslim managed minority educational institutions.

Special thanks are due to Dr. (Mrs) Mary Parmar (Shimla) for her missionary zeal with which she complied with my request for providing whatever information she could collect about the Buddhist institutions. Without her support this study would have suffered a serious gap. It would have been difficult to get complete details of the Buddhist educational institutions as they were scattered in different parts of India, and no attempt was made to organize them under one umbrella organization.

To Arnavaz Mama, F.J. Antia, Mrs. R.E. Mehta, R.A. Lalkaka, we owe a great deal for providing copious details and information about the Parsi educational institutions.

The invaluable assistance and cooperation given by Delhi Sikh Management Committee through the kindness and generosity of their President Shri S. Rajinder Singh Monga cannot be adequately measured by words of thanks. Without his support it would be extremely difficult to go into the Sikh educational institutions.

The Church of North India through their detailed publications, guidelines and discussions highlighted the problems of the Christian managed educational institutions. Father Joseph, General Secretary, All India Association of Catholic Educational Institutions, CBCI Centre, Delhi, deserves mention for the benefit of discussion and guidance.

We cannot forget the assistance given by Dr Balwant Singh, Coordinator, TOC, Punjabi University, Patiala, in collecting questionnaires from different areas in Punjab. Authorities of the various monasteries, churches, mosques, gurudwaras and Anjumans deserve appreciation for their cooperation.

Numerous institutions, their heads, members of the management committees, teaching and non-teaching staff, parents, leaders of the local community, students, government officials whose collective efforts have gone equally into the making of this book, deserve our thanks.

Particular mention may be made of Mohammad Zafar Saifullah, former Secretary, Minorities Commission and former Cabinet Secretary, and Ashok Pahwa (now Secretary, Government of India), A.K. Rastogi former Joint Secretaries, Minorities Commission, for their support; to the authorities of the IIPA;

former Directors, Shri T.N. Chaturvedi, presently Chairman, Standing Committee of IIPA, and Member of Parliament; Shri G.C.L. Joneja, Shri P.K. Umashankar, Shri B.C. Mathur, Shri Manik Wadhwani and present Director, Shri M.C. Gupta, my thanks are due.

My thanks are also due to Prof. Dr. Horst F. Rolly of the University of Friedensau who has been working on a research project on "Educational Rights and Educational Practices of Religious and Linguistic Minorities in India" of Heidelberg University, Germany in collaboration with Prof. Dr. Lenhart for discussion on this subject.

Shri S. Majumdar, deputy librarian, Mrs. S. Bakshi, Shri D. Kumar, Shri A.K. Joshi, Shri A.K. Nath, (assistant librarians) deserve appreciation for library services; and Mrs Sunita Gulati of IIPA library for bibliographic assistance.

Shri S. Parthiban, Mrs A.A. Shrivastava, Shri Girish Joshi, Mrs. Daman Arora who assisted in various ways, deserve appreciation.

My special thanks are due to Mr B.P. Garg, Managing Director, and Mr Amit Garg, Director of Gyan Publishing House, without whose untiring zeal and efforts the book would not have seen the light in such good shape.

R.N. Thakur

Terms Explained

Grievance

(i) In labour law, a complaint filed by an employee or by his or her union representative, regarding working conditions and for resolution of which there is procedural machinery provided in the Union Contract; an injury, injustice or wrong which gives ground for complaint because it is unjust, discriminatory and oppressive.

(*Black's Law Dictionary*, Sixth Edition, 1991, p. 702).

(ii) The infliction of wrong or hardship on a person; injury, oppression; a cause or source of injury.
The state or fact of being oppressed, injured, or distressed; trouble, distress; suffering, pain.
Circumstance or state of things which is felt to be oppressive. In modern use, a wrong or hardship (real or supposed) which is considered a legitimate ground of complaint; something to complain of.

(*The Oxford Dictionary*, Vol. VI, 1989, pp. 835-36).

(iii) In this study, 'grievance' has been explained in the following words:
The grievances are the sum of accumulated strain resulting from certain stress situations.

Minority

Minority is explained in the following words:
A group of people in a given society who, because of their distinct physical or cultural characteristics, find themselves

in situations of inequality within that society.

A group which is perceived as such (minority) by other groups.

In India, minority has become a political term, with a political tinge.

Minority, in this study, includes the religious minority, like, the Buddhists, the Christians, the Muslims, the Parsis, and the Sikhs.

List of Tables

PART I

CONCEPTUAL AND CONSTITUTIONAL ASPECTS

Exploring into the concept of the minority from sociological, psychological, political, geographical, demographic, legal, constitutional stand-point in historical and comparative global context, in order to concretize the concept in the Indian perspective by reducing its vagueness, is a challenging task.

ONE

Introduction: Methodology

The grievances are the sum of accumulated strain resulting from the financial and non-financial stress situations on the part of the minority managed educational institutions which have to be shared by management, the heads of the institutions, teaching and non-teaching staff as well as the students. Their impact is also felt by the local community, the leaders, the parents, the governmental functionary and the nation at large. Problems and grievances in the minority education remained a hitherto neglected area. They need utmost attention.

Education plays a catalytic role in the development of a community or country. Ever since the attainment of independence, efforts have been made to prepare a plan of educational development for India. At the unofficial level, there has been considerable development of ideas resulting in a sociology of education in which the centrality of educational systems to the structure and the functioning of pre-agriculture to post-industrial societies has attained an important place. Education which was seen as essential for every member of civilized society to manifest his/her roles and duties effectively was reviewed as being functionally linked to economic growth and social change.

At the official level, there were several committees and commissions appointed at various periods to review the education system after independence. The Central Advisory Board of Education, the oldest and the most important advisory body of the Government of India on education was established in 1920 and revived in 1935 after a brief period of suspension. This Board with the union minister of education as its chairman, from time to time reviewed several aspects of education and adopted resolutions in its annual meetings.

The Education Ministry's first conference was initiated in 1949 by the then Education Minister Abul Kalam Azad. Among other things the conference also considered measures to be adopted for the solution of crucial problems in education.

In 1964, the Education Commission was appointed under the Chairmanship of Dr D.S. Kothari to advise the Union Government on the national pattern of education and on the policies for development of education.

Several committees were set up to review and analyse the different aspects of education. Unfortunately none of these committees had any comprehensive agenda on religious minorities' education and the attempts were to view the problems of minorities' education in comparison with general education.

Due to the absence of any coherent attempt in any of the various commissions, committees and panels appointed by the Central and State Governments from time to time, minorities' education remained at the crossroads. No clear-cut policy or guidelines were framed to regulate the education for minorities without contravening the basic tenets of the constitutional provisions for this section of the Indian population.

Both the National Policy on Education of 1968 and 1986 made passing references to minorities' education in their aims to promote national progress and sense of culture and national integration. The only notable reference to minorities' education in the National Policy on Education, 1986 was,

> *Some minority groups are educationally deprived or backward. Greater attention will be paid to the education of these groups in the interest of equality and social justice. This naturally includes the constitutional guarantees given to them to establish and administer educational institutions and protection to their language and culture. Simultaneously, objectivity will be reflected in the preparation of textbooks and in all school activities, and all possible measures will be taken to promote an integration based on appreciation of common national goals and ideals, in conformity with the core curriculum.*

However, this reference had only a limited purpose in the

sense that the programme of action in order to implement the national policy on education, and in order to pursue 'point no. 11 of the Prime Minister's 15-point programme' regarding the integration of the minorities in all walks of life suggested only guidelines on coaching classes for competitive examinations for weaker sections amongst educationally backward minorities. Hence, even the highest national document on education did not pronounce any policy guidelines on minorities' education.

An overall appraisal of the situation, planning and management of the minorities' education on an all India basis with the terms and references applied in the commissions and committees held so far, is inadequate to ensure the proper maintenance of minorities' education.

Minorities' educational institutions are pitted against several problems today in their effort to exercise their right of establishing and administering their own institutions.

The mere constitutional provisions to "establish and administer" institutions of their own choice now had acquired reasonable restrictions, in that the state has the right to provide regulatory provisions for ensuring educational excellence, conditions of employment of teachers, ensuring health, hygiene and discipline and allied matters. Such measures are purported to ensure that minorities' institutions are administered efficiently and that the students who come out of minority institutions are well equipped with knowledge and training so as to stand at par in their avocation in life without any handicap.

If the minority institution seeks affiliation or recognition from the state, the state has the right to prescribe syllabi and terms and conditions for giving such affiliation or recognition or extending grants-in-aid.

Hence, between the pressures of the constitutional provisions and reasonable restrictions by State Governments to ensure the quality of education for minorities arise the grievances of management of the minority institutions. These grievances generally are the result of two different views both of which, however, have the same intended purpose — provision of education of their own choice to minorities in India.

The grievances of the management range from proving the

minority status of an institution, to the affiliation, appointments of staff, admission of students, school buildings and grants-in-aid from the various government agencies.

Despite the constitutional provisions, and five decades of subsequent efforts of the government at every level, the educational development, has still a long way to go. This slow pace is a threat to one-fourth of India's population, i.e., minorities. The Plan expenditure on education in India registered a substantial rise since the inception of Five-Year Plan. The central allocation for the First Plan was Rs 153 crore which rose to Rs 5,457 crore in Seventh Plan, and Rs 7,443 crore in Eighth Five-Year Plan. Increasingly larger amounts of resources are being allocated for education. The funds spent for the development of minorities' education in absence of statistics even with the best deal would not be more than their proportion to the total population.

Though increasingly larger amounts of resources are being allocated to education, the share of educational sector in the total plan outlay has been consistently declining from 7.8% in the First Plan to 2.8% in the Sixth Plan. A slight increase was noticed in the Seventh Five-Year Plan in which 3.03% of the total outlay was made, and which was brought down to 3% of total outlay in Eighth Five-Year Plan. Government educational expenditures increased from 2.6% of GDP in 1976-77 to 3.4% in 1986-87. Yet, it is much less than those in many other developing countries, such as, Thailand 4.2%; Malaysia 8.5%; and Kenya 4.2%. A break-up of intra-sectoral allocation of resources in education in India during the different five-year plans would show a lopsided emphasis on different levels of education.

The different states and local bodies which also spend on education had also considerably increased their respective allocation. However, the inhibition to the development of education in general, and minorities' education in particular, partially contributed to the slow rate of growth of governments' expenditures on education, and the situation has been further complicated by ever increasing population in its numerical size.

The minorities' educational institutions taking support from the constitutional provisions are rapidly increasing to cope up with the population growth. Hence, more and more institutions compete for less and less government funds in real terms.

The mere constitutional provision of "establishing and administration of educational institutions of their own choice" will not guarantee the funds from various government bodies, and the fact is that these minority institutions have to compete with other General Institutions in terms of the procedures, rules, regulations and standards set in different places in different ways. This gives scope for accumulation of grievances which are financial in nature at the institutional level.

Besides the financial problem, educational institutions in general, and minority institutions in particular, face numerous other problems in building an institution.

The first main problem apart from grants-in-aid, is the lack of infrastructure facilities in these institutions. Sufficient number of classrooms, toilet, water, laboratory, library and playground facilities which are considered to be minimum requirements, are not often available to them.

An educational survey conducted by the Hamdard Education Society revealed that Muslim educational institutions by and large lack physical facilities, have non-availability of trained teachers apart from many other problems. There are also other grievances of teaching and non-teaching staff regarding their payment and service conditions, etc.

This study relates to the conceptual and constitutional aspect of the minorities as well as the problems and grievances in their education, particularly, financial and non-financial grievances of the minority managed educational institutions. Five principal areas in which these grievances could be located have been identified.

In order to evolve the pattern of grievances, the opinions of the following personnel at the institution were recorded in the study:

(i) Management members
(ii) Heads of the institutions
(iii) Teaching Staff
(iv) Non-Teaching Staff
(v) Students

Besides, these, the following were also included:

(vi) Government functionaries (mostly of education department)

(vii) Community leaders
(viii) Political and opinion leaders

Objective of the Study:

The study has following objectives:

(i) To know about the different sources of funds for the institution;
(ii) To know about the adequacy or inadequacy; and delay in the release of funds;
(iii) To know about the areas affected due to inadequate grants; and delay in the release of funds;
(iv) To know about the grievances related to payment, non-payment or underpayment, and incentives or non-incentives;
(v) To know about the scholarships and monetary benefits for students.

The book has been divided into three parts (Conceptual and Constitutional Aspects, Financial Grievances and Non-Financial and other Grievances) with the following chapters:

1. Introduction: Methodology

This chapter presents a discussion on the background of problems of minorities' education both at the levels of policy and institutions, and the contents of the study as well as methodology.

2. Concept of Minority

The word 'minority' is used in different meanings in different contexts. This chapter presents a global view of the minorities. A detailed discussion on this concept has been made from sociological, demographic and constitutional points of view, and an attempt has been made to define 'minority' in precise terms.

3. Constitutional Provisions and Judicial Pronouncements on Educational Rights of the Minorities

In this chapter a detailed discussion is made on the constitutional provisions for minorities; and several court cases interpreting the provisions in different contexts.

4. An Analysis of the Minority Managed Educational Institutions

It gives the details of the minority managed educational institutions of various types studied in depth, time gap between their establishment and recognition, teacher-student ratio, infrastructural facilities available, etc.

5. Financial Grievances of the Minority Managed Educational Institutions

This chapter throws light on the financial grievances of the minority managed educational institutions. The analysis is based on the information collected through mainly primary sources and also secondary sources to some extent. The financial grievances are analysed in three forms: (i) statewise; (ii) religionwise; and (iii) institutionwise.

6. Financial Grievances Aggregated

This chapter presents a detailed summary of financial grievances aggregated together statewise based on the response by the respondents.

Some grievances are common and universal but some are specific to a particular state situation.

7. Conclusion: Outcome and Recommendations

Any situational analysis is not of much use unless it suggests measures to remedy the situation. A detailed discussion on the outcome and recommendations is done at the end.

8. Non-Financial Grievances of the Minority Managed Educational Institutions

This chapter, based on data collected from the field and through mailed questionnaires, discusses the non-financial grievances of minority managed educational institutions.

9. Minority Organizations and Institutions in the Field of Education: Some Case-Studies

This chapter presents some case-studies of Muslim, Christian and Parsi organizations and institutions. How they developed and contributed to the cause of minorities' education, whether they could be emulated by other minority organizations and institutions.

10. Non-Financial and other Grievances of Minority Managed Educational Institutions Aggregated

This chapter presents statewise an overview of the non-financial and other grievances of the minority managed educational institutions, some grievances are common and universal but some are specific to a particular state situation.

11. Conclusion: Outcome and Recommendations

In order to remedy the situation, a detailed discussion on the suggestions and recommendations is provided for policy decisions in this regard.

Appendices

In appendices, tables and charts are included.

Methodology

1. Objectives of the Study
2. Area of the Study
3. Period of the Study
4. Limitations of the Study
5. Selection of Samples
6. Collection of Data
   - (i) Primary Data Collection
     - (a) Discussions with Government Officials
     - (b) Discussions with Central and State Minorities Commissions/Boards
     - (c) Discussions with Management Members
     - (d) Discussions with Minority Community Organizations/Leaders/Political Leaders.
   - (ii) Secondary Data Collection
7. Questionnaire/Interview Schedule
8. Schedule of Analysis

Objectives of the Study

No piece of research stands alone. One research study may easily lead to another because it raises issues which the researcher had not previously considered. The point is whether the previous research study has already satisfactorily clarified the problem. In the area of the grievances of the minority managed educational institutions no research study was previously attempted. Hence, clear formulation of research problem is the basic task for this research.

Therefore, the present study was designed with the following broad objectives:

(i) To study the nature and types of grievances of the minority managed educational institutions;

(ii) To identify the causes of their grievances;

(iii) To analyse the perception of various categories, such as, the members of the managing committees, teaching and non-teaching staff, students, parents, local community and governmental functionaries about the grievances;

(iv) To analyse the various consequences of these grievances in different areas, such as:

  (a) Management of the educational institutions;

  (b) Conducting teaching and other academic and co-curricular activities effectively;

  (c) Drop out among the students;

  (d) Disincentive to teachers, etc.

(v) To compare the minority managed educational institutions as regards their grievances *vis-a-vis* the other institutions in the area, to identify the peculiarity of the grievance of the minority managed institutions;

(vi) And to suggest short-term and long-term remedies to grievances redressal.

The results are incorporated in Parts II and III of the book. Part II is related to the study of the financial grievances; and Part III deals with the non-financial and other grievances of the minority managed educational institutions.

Area of the Study

The study was conducted to assess the varying nature, extent, type, and causes of:

(a) financial grievances, and

(b) non-financial grievances of the minority managed educational institutions in selected states and union territories.

The problems and grievances of the minority institutions were the focus of attention.

On the basis of concentration of minority population, and minority managed educational institutions in various states, the following states were selected for the study:

1. Andhra Pradesh
2. Bihar
3. Chandigarh
4. Delhi
5. Gujarat
6. Haryana
7. Himachal Pradesh
8. Karnataka
9. Kerala
10. Madhya Pradesh
11. Maharashtra
12. Mizoram
13. Orissa
14. Punjab
15. Rajasthan
16. Tamil Nadu
17. Uttar Pradesh
18. West Bengal

Period of the Study

The duration of the study is more than one year from July 1991 to September 1992. The secondary data collection was done regularly between July 1991 to September 1991, and intermittently afterwards till the end. The field investigations were done between October 1991 to May 1992. The questionnaires were mailed and generally received after July 1992, filled in between October 1991 to June 1992. Between July 1992 and October 1992, data analysis was done manually as well as by the aid of computers. By December 1992, the details of the financial and non-financial grievances of the minority managed educational institutions in India had been finalized.

The study had not been restricted to any specific year. The grievances relevant to the current period in the minorities' institutions have been focused.

Limitations of the Study

The study has limited itself to two basic issues:

(i) Financial grievances, and
(ii) Non-financial and other grievances of the minority managed educational institutions in India.

These two aspects were the focus of the research though data was collected from various kinds of institutions, Organizations and individuals. In addition, the ways of removing the bottlenecks, and improving the situation and identifying policy priorities were also part of this study. The study has limited itself to only problems and grievances of the minority managed educational institutions and not any other institutions owned by the minorities, or educational institutions that are managed by others.

The study suffered certain limitations in field visits. The correct perspective of different persons associated with the schools and colleges was difficult to obtain in some places, and it became almost impossible in some other places. For instance, in some cases the management of the institution, or head of the institution were not willing to let our team carry out the work planned, or let anyone from their institution reveal any information whatsoever. Field notes were meticulously kept; recording each day's activities. Sometimes some curious situations were faced.

The principal of a college was unwilling to give interview, denied permission to have interview with his staff; faculty and staff were scared of the principal, and were not willing to give any information. The principal on persuasion reluctantly took the questionnaire, had a look at it, and threw it off saying that he had 'no time to answer'.

When the President of the Prabandhak Committee was approached, and he circulated a letter of introduction, some interviews could be done, several questionnaires could be filled. 'They don't have time' - such answers were not an uncommon experience in many places.

In several cases, the principal arranged to give reply on behalf of the staff and teachers. At other places group interviews were also arranged.

We attempted to study the grievances from the points of view of:

(i) The management,
(ii) The head of the institution,
(iii) The teachers,
(iv) The non-teaching staff,
(v) The students,
(vi) Community and opinion leaders,
(vii) The parents, and
(viii) The government functionaries.

But it was not always possible to make the study from the points of view of all the groups of people connected with the minority managed educational institutions. Yet, the fieldwork provided much richer source of information.

We used representative sampling as well as random sampling in the research. Samples were selected from various states and districts, keeping in mind the concentration of the minority population, and the minority managed educational institutions, i.e., primary, secondary, college, general type, technical and professional.

Selection of Samples

The total number of samples selected for this study was 535. The samples were selected randomly on the basis of minority population in the districts and states. The final selection of samples was done as below:

(i) At first, States and Union Territories for field visits were identified.
(ii) Then it was grouped into two ways, that is, (a) on the basis of the concentration of population belonging to different religions at the district level and, (b) the concentration of minority managed educational institutions in various districts of those selected States and Union Territories.

On the basis of population distribution of different religious minorities the following size of samples was initially decided for each group:

(i)	Muslim managed educational institutions	300
(ii)	Christian managed educational institutions	75
(iii)	Sikh managed educational institutions	60
(iv)	Parsi managed educational institutions	25
(v)	Buddhist managed educational institutions	25

Though the final number of samples in each category and their total varied because of different reasons, yet the proportion which was decided was largely kept undisturbed.

All religious group samples were further divided into the type of Institutions, and accordingly, following were the final distributions of samples as shown in Table 1.1.

TABLE - 1.1
DISTRIBUTION OF SAMPLES

*(Total samples — 535)**

Type of Institutions	*Muslim Managed*	*Christian Managed*	*Sikh Managed*	*Parsi Managed*	*Buddhist Managed*
Total Samples	310	70	70	55	30
Primary Schools	56	5	0	15	5
Upper Primary Schools	16	5	0	10	5
Secondary Schools	68	10	10	45	15
Higher Secondary Schools	90	25	10	0	0
Pre-university Inter Colleges	15	0	5	0	0
Graduate Colleges	34	5	30	5	5
Postgraduate Colleges	25	20	15	0	0
Professional and Technical Institutes	6	0*	0*	0*	0

Note: *The actual number of samples included in the study is slightly more than 535 with the inclusion of 2 Christian Professional Institutions, 2 Sikh Professional Institutions, and one Parsi Technical Institution. The details from these institutions reached us rather late when tables were already finalized. However, the data from these questionnaires have been used by incorporating them in the detailed analysis.

While there was no hard and fast rule applied in selecting the number of institutions in each type, the size of samples in each type of institutions was adjusted in relation to the concentration of such institution in various areas.

The Statewise distribution of the samples is given below:

1.	Andhra Pradesh	25
2.	Bihar	5
3.	Chandigarh	15
4.	Delhi	20
5.	Gujarat	30
6.	Haryana	5
7.	Karnataka	100
8.	Kerala	45
9.	Maharashtra	85
10.	Mizoram	20
11.	Orissa	15
12.	Punjab	45
13.	Tamil Nadu	55
14.	Uttar Pradesh	60
15.	West Bengal	10
	Total	535
	(Himachal Pradesh, Madhya Pradesh, Rajasthan included)	

Due to practical difficulties the even distribution of samples was not possible statewise. The differential sampling in each state simply reflects the differential response showed to the survey.

Collection of Data

For the purpose of giving wider publicity and to obtain more reliable data from minorities institutions, correspondence was done from three different levels.

I. The Minorities Commission, Government of India, communicated letters to various State Governments and U.T. Administration, Minorities Commissions and Boards of the States which further spread the message to the districts, and lower levels in their respective areas.

II. State Governments, State Minorities Commissions and Boards were approached for furnishing details on financial and non-financial grievances of the minority managed educational institutions.

III. The Project Director communicated to various State Governments and State Minorities Commissions. The correspondences were regularly carried out with educational institutions, individuals associated with institutions, individuals from academia, politics, various professions, community leaders, government officials and non-governmental organizations. The main emphasis was on institutions. More than 1500 questionnaires were mailed to them and follow up action was regularly taken. Three reminders, in general, at an interval of approximately one month were sent for the return of the questionnaires.

In many cases, the institutions, the management, the officials, the ministers and legislators approached us on their own for copies of questionnaires. We meticulously tried to comply with the request in almost all cases in which the requests were made. Altogether approximately 35 per cent questionnaires were received back sooner or later.

Primary Data Collection

For the purpose of primary data collection, it was necessary to have an exhaustive list of the minority managed educational institutions in India to select samples from various states and religious groups. As a first step to the primary data collection, a comprehensive list of the minority managed educational institutions was procured from several sources for all religions. The list was procured from 21 States and Union Territories in India. This list was scrutinized and reorganized. They were classified statewise which in turn was classified according to religious group. These religious groups were further classified into various types of institutions for every religion under each state.

In order to procure the list and to give wider publicity for field investigation for the sake of awareness of the minority institutions, and in order to elicit cooperation for the investigating team, various journals and organizations were approached in an effort to bring out a press-release. About fifteen national dailies and journals published the details in English and Urdu, which include:

(i) Fana
(ii) Dawat
(iii) Urdu Times
(iv) Daily Salar (24th Dec. 1991)
(v) Quami Awaz (19th Dec. 1991)
(vi) Parsiana (Jan. 1992)
(vii) The Deccan Herald (25th Feb. 1992)
(viii) The Indian Express (25th Feb. 1992)
(ix) The Islamic Voice
(x) Minorities Commission News Quarterly
(xi) Kanti.

Apart from these, more than one thousand institutions and organizations were communicated through correspondence; and questionnaires along with instructions mailed to them.

The original list compiled was rather exhaustive and it was short-listed for the purpose of field visit, and an appropriate plan was envisaged for field visit to cover maximum places in minimum duration and expenditures. The places from where the samples were collected through interview schedules are as follows:

(i)	Andhra Pradesh	-	(a) Hyderabad
			(b) Secunderabad
(ii)	Bihar	-	(a) Bhagalpur
			(b) Patna
(iii)	Chandigarh	-	Chandigarh
(iv)	Delhi	-	Delhi
(v)	Gujarat	-	Ahmedabad
(vi)	Haryana	-	(a) Gurgaon
			(b) Hisar
			(c) Kurukshetra
(vii)	Karnataka	-	(a) Bangalore
			(b) Gulbarga
			(c) Shimoga
			(d) Hassan
			(e) Ankola
			(f) Mysore

(viii) Kerala	-	(a) Ernakulam (b) Cochin (c) Malappuram (d) Thiruvananthapuram (e) Calicut (f) Trichur
(ix) Maharashtra	-	(a) Mumbai (b) Pune (c) Nagpur (d) Buldana (e) Malegaon (f) Aurangabad (g) Nasik
(x) Mizoram	-	Champhai
(xi) Orissa	-	Phulbani
(xii) Punjab	-	(a) Chandigarh (b) Ludhiana
(xiii) Rajasthan	-	Jaipur
(xiv) Tamil Nadu	-	(a) Thanjavur (b) Chennai
(xv) Uttar Pradesh	-	(a) Meerut (b) Ghaziabad (c) Lucknow (d) Varanasi (e) Saranath (f) Basti
(xvi) West Bengal	-	(a) Calcutta (b) Darjeeling

At the initial phase, a pilot survey was conducted in Delhi as soon as the questionnaire was ready. Based on the observations in Delhi, slight modifications were done in the questionnaires.

In the second phase, 4 Southern States were chosen. Accordingly, in this phase with the help of state minorities commissions and other concerned government officials our research team was sent to conduct survey in Tamil Nadu, Kerala and Karnataka. Another team did the survey in Andhra Pradesh simultaneously.

Fieldwork was simultaneously continuing in Delhi and adjoining areas in the vicinity of Delhi.

In the third phase, an extensive survey in Delhi covering Muslim, Sikh, Buddhist and Christian institutions was conducted, while at the same time, the survey was also conducted in Ghaziabad, Meerut (Uttar Pradesh) and Gurgaon (Haryana).

The States of Maharashtra, Mizoram, Orissa, Punjab, Uttar Pradesh and West Bengal were covered in the fourth phase, while in the final phase, Bihar, some parts of Uttar Pradesh, and Rajasthan were covered.

Discussion with Government Officials

In the field visits, besides data collection from the educational institutions, the government officials were consulted and detailed discussions were held in order to study the problem in depth. The following organizations were consulted almost in every state for detailed discussions on the various problems:

(i) Directorate of Public Instruction/Commissioner of Education at State Capitals.
(ii) Directorate of Secondary and Higher Secondary Education at State Capitals.
(iii) Directorate of Collegiate Education at State Capitals.
(iv) Office of Deputy Director, Education in various regions.
(v) District Education Office in various Districts.
(vi) Directorate of Minorities Education/Zila Parishad Office

In the states wherever field visits were done, the respective State Minorities Commissions were contacted personally in order to understand regional problems and to ensure their co-operation for field visit. The notable ones were:

(a) The State Minorities Commission, Patna (Bihar).
(b) The State Minorities Commission, Bangalore (Karnataka).
(c) The State Minorities Commission, Madras (Tamil Nadu).
(d) The State Minorities Commission, Lucknow (Uttar Pradesh).
(e) The Minorities Welfare Board, Jaipur (Rajasthan).

Some of these Commissions accorded their assistance for useful discussions with various organizations and institutions apart from supplying some relevant materials.

Discussions with Management Members

Most of the institutions investigated personally included detailed discussions with their management. The Management of these Institutions were informed through correspondence about the details of the study and field visits and they were contacted in the field. Besides collecting information through interview schedule, detailed discussions, and in some cases, group discussions in free atmosphere were conducted to comprehend the problems in their real nature. This was also done with an intention to bring cordial atmosphere for field investigation team at the Institution. In most of the cases, discussions with these members were useful as they held important positions in the community, or, in the field of education, whose fruitful experience is an added advantage for an indepth analysis.

Discussions with Minority Community Leaders/Organization/Politicians

Several voluntary organizations and others engaged in the socio-economic and educational development of religious minorities in India were consulted. They are in day-to-day contact with minorities' educational institutions. These organizations were contacted through correspondence and their opinions and suggestions were obtained on the problems of minorities institutions. Several organizations have also been contacted during field investigations and their assistance was made available.

Several community leaders and politicians were also personally contacted in order to study the problems from various angles. Being local and influential leaders of community, and as their representatives many of them were up-to-date with regard to government policies and programmes. The discussions with them were useful in identifying the loopholes of policies and programmes launched in different regions for the development and improvement of standards of education in the minorities' institutions.

Secondary Data Collection

The initial effort in this study started with collecting information through secondary sources, through several official documents available on the subject in order to grasp the subject in depth. Though they are included in the bibliography, it becomes necessary to mention a few which were our basic readings in understanding the different issues. They were:

(a) Government Documents
  (i) Constitution of India
  (ii) The Constituent Assembly Debates Vols. I-II, IV, VI-VIII
  (iii) Annual Reports of the Ministry of Welfare and Minorities Commission

(b) Press clippings on various issues and problems of Minority Institutions

(c) Relevant Books and Articles on the subject.

Questionnaire/Interview Schedule

Questionnaire having standardized set of questions, and also open-ended questions were used. Questions were carefully constructed so as to elicit correct, and more and more information while giving freedom of choice.

Schedules were carefully designed in relation to the characteristics of the respondents. The research study was preceded by a pilot study in order to pick up problems not anticipated by us.

Questionnaire-cum-interview schedule prepared for this study in 34 pages were divided into four parts.

Schedule of Analysis

The analysis for financial and non-financial grievances of the minority managed educational institutions are as follows:

(a) Institution Data Schedule which is based on the following:
  (i) Institutions on the basis of grant-in-aid
  (ii) Institutions under different Religion and State.
  (iii) Time-gap between year of establishment and recognition of the Institution.

(iv) Teacher-student ratio in Institutions of various types.
(v) Infrastructure facilities of Institutions.
(vi) Vocational advantage/disadvantage of the Institution.
(vii) Co-curricular activities of the Institution.

(b) Analysis on Financial Grievances

The analysis of financial grievances is mainly based on information from three different sources: (a) Management (b) Teaching staff (c) Students. The analysis is categorized into following groups:

(i) Analysis on Institutions of different religions.
(ii) Analysis on Minority Institutions of different States/ Union Territories.
(iii) Analysis on Minority Institutions of different types.

The following analysis has been made separately for each group mentioned above.

(a) Source of financial grants-in-aid
(b) Perception of management with regard to financial grievances in respect of:
 (i) Adequacy of grants
 (ii) Delay in distribution of grants
 (iii) Areas affected due to delay in release of grants
 - Salaries of the staff
 - Maintenance of the building
 - Scholarships
 - Teaching aids
 - Sports activities
(c) Perception of Head of the Institution with regard to financial grievances in respect of:
 (i) Utilization of grants
 (ii) Adequacy of grants
(d) Perception of teaching staff with regard to suggestions for development on minority managed educational institutions.

Analysis on non-financial grievances related to:

(i) The problems of official recognition;
(ii) perception of management about adequacy of various facilities;

(iii) grievances of teaching staff regarding
   (a) Pay
   (b) Incentives
   (c) Allowances
   (d) Teaching/Training/Housing Facilities
   (e) Medical Facilities

(iv) perception of teaching staff about the attitude of
   (a) Management
   (b) Head of the Institution
   (c) Colleagues
   (d) Non-Teaching Staff
   (e) Students
   (f) Parents
   (g) Government functionaries

(v) the perception of teaching staff about the reasons of lack of motivation among students; and

(vi) rating of students over the facilities in their institution.

Besides these, the study is also directed towards the grievances redressal; and case-study of some Institutions/Organizations.

The book is based on a systematic and scientific analysis of facts obtained from the field through mailed questionnaire, interview-schedule, objective observation and discussion. Both the documentary and the field sources have been extensively tapped. We used the survey method, results have been quantified and analysed statistically with the aid of electronic calculator and also computer. The survey research was time-consuming, but there was no escape as we had to cover various states and union territories. We did not make an in-depth study of a particular state or district.

In the mailed questionnaire there was some difficulty on account of the use of English. This difficulty was more felt at primary levels, especially in Hindi-speaking belts.

However, the survey research findings were supplemented by field research and face-to-face interview.

In fact, we used a process called triangulation in this research combining several methods of research, such as, survey method, field study, questionnaire, interview, etc., using each to supplement and check upon others.

TWO

Concept of Minority

Various communities in India have lived together for centuries; although they have followed different religious faiths and beliefs, yet they occasionally regard one another with hostility or disdain.

The interventionist policy of some of the Mughal rulers, and divide-and-rule policy of the British rulers created a gap among the communities which became accentuated over a period of time. India's Constitution introduced the term 'minority' and incorporated special provisions for the minority in its various Articles, such as, 29, 30, etc. Although the Constitution of India gave equal rights to all citizens, yet, some special provisions were laid down for the minorities, perhaps, treating them as disadvantaged and socially isolated communities. But, the same is not true of all the minority communities. The Muslims generally remained concentrated in distinct neighbourhoods in both rural and urban areas; the Buddhists as many of them belong to the hilly regions and tribal groups had their own distinct neighbourhoods; the Neo-Buddhists, a great many of whom were converts from low Hindu caste categories, maintained their own distinct entity in terms of residence; the Parsis were different from other groups as they were confined to particular territories in mainly urban areas; the Sikhs shared commonness in neighbourhoods in terms of residence; the Muslims maintained an entirely distinct entity; so also the Christians, even if, they were converts.

Intermarriages within these communities were generally considered as bringing disgrace on the family, and a threat to particular religious identity.

Within a country that has risen to become a modern democracy with equal rights, opportunities, freedom and liberty to all citizens; some of the communities form minority communities with feeling of separateness, at times, hostility or disdain.

The intermarriages within these communities remained strictly restricted. In spite of the Constitutional provisions of equality in the eye of law, social prejudice and discrimination continued to remain strong in case of some of them.

In their rites, rituals and practices, in forms of worship and prayers and in food habits these communities maintained differences.

Minorities in a Plural Society

Even when there are no physical differences in the people of these communities, yet prejudices are ingrained and enduring. The Jews have been subjected to persecution in the Christian world of the West for about two thousand years; the most horrific instance of brutal destructiveness against a minority group being the killing of millions of Jews in German Concentration Camps during the Second World War.

The recent horrific tale of wanton destructiveness inflicted on the Serbs (Muslims) (by Croats) in Yugoslavia has completely exposed the hollowness of the so-called civilized world of the West in the age of human rights during the last decade of the twentieth century.

Members of ethnic groups see themselves as culturally distinct from other groupings in a society.

Many different characteristics distinguish ethnic groups from one another, but the most usual are religion, styles of dress, or adornment, ancestry or history (real or imagined) or language.

Many societies in the industrialized and relatively less industrialized world today are plural societies. In these plural societies, several large groupings, involved in the same economic and political order, are living largely distinct from one another. It is generally held that most of the post-colonial countries are pluralistic societies, because of the political unification imposed on a variety of pre-existing cultures.

The case of India is somewhat different. Here, the various communities like the Hindus, the Muslims, the Sikhs, the Christians, the Buddhists and the Parsis are living together for centuries with a bond of unity of culture and tradition. There are large groups of converts. These groups in spite of their distinct language, and practices, and religion, mix together and also combine. The resurgence of the saintly tradition of India brings them together into a typical common Indian heritage. It is not merely economic and political unification, it is unification into a combination through common cultural heritage of dance, drama, music, and a deeply divine faith and belief. In spite of differences and conflicts, the Indian people live together and combine into a unity which often inspires this nation in the event of a national crisis and threat of a war.

If this is so, then: Is the notion of minority associated with inequality of opportunity, power and wealth? Is it associated with antagonism between groups? Is it an instrument of political use? What accounts for prejudices and discrimination between the minority group and other groupings?

Sociological Interpretation

The notion of minority groups is widely used in sociology, and involves more than mere numbers. Minorities in a statistical sense are not the minorities in sociological terms.

In sociological terms, a minority group has the following three distinct features:

(i) The members of a minority group are disadvantaged as a result of discrimination against them by others. Discrimination arises when rights and opportunities open to one set of people are denied to another group.

The question arises whether the minority groups in India are denied those rights and opportunities that are open to the other groupings? The Constitution of India guarantees equal rights and opportunities to all citizens. Therefore, the question of denial of rights and opportunities in constitutional term to a minority group does not arise. It is a different matter how far certain rights and opportunities are availed by a particular group; how far they have access to these rights and opportunities. A group which is weak in terms of education, wealth and power is not likely to have access to the rights and opportunities given to them under the Constitution. Hence, the members of the group remain disadvantaged although there is no discrimination against them.

Then the other point is whether the group has awareness of those rights and opportunities; whether their perception about them is clear. Whether they compare their own positions vis-à-vis other groups. Whether they remain socially, educationally, economically disadvantaged. These points apply as much to the members of the minority group as to those of any other groups.

(ii) Secondly, the members of the minority have some sense of group solidarity, of 'belonging together'. Their experience of being the subject of prejudice and discrimination usually heightens feelings of common loyalty and interests. Members of minority groups often tend to see themselves as 'a people apart' from the majority. This is, to some extent, true of the minorities in India.

(iii) Thirdly, the minority groups are to some extent physically and socially isolated from the larger community. They tend to be concentrated in certain neighbourhoods in rural and urban areas.

There is only some case of intermarriage between these groupings. Marriage within the group itself is always promoted in order to keep alive their cultural distinctiveness.

It has also been suggested that since the notion is sociological rather than numerical, a minority group might, in certain circumstances, consist of the majority of the population. In South Africa, a relatively small proportion of whites dominate much larger number of blacks. The use of the term 'minority' in such circumstances seems a little contradictory, and even confusing.

The minority groups are always to some degree ethnically distinct from the majority.

Many minorities are both ethnically and physically distinct from the rest of the population of the societies in which they live. This is the case with West Indians and Asians in Britain; and with American Indians, Chinese and certain other groups in the USA.

It must be clearly understood that the racial prejudice and discrimination of the Western type does not exist in India, in the case of the minorities. No doubt, some of the religious minorities, such as, the Buddhists, and the Muslims suffer disadvantage in terms of education, opportunity, wealth and power; while the other minorities, such as, the Christians, the Sikhs, and the Parsis are not similarly circumstanced. In spite of their number being small, the Sikhs remain dominant, and in the forefront, in business, profession and entrepreneurship; the Christians are relatively more developed and upward looking in education and profession.

Considered from one angle, the minority is a fluid concept, at times contradictory and even confusing. Often one is led to believe that the concept of minority should be dropped altogether.

Looked at from another angle, such as, preserving ones racial stock, cultural heritage, tradition, and language, the concept of minority appears to be real; it should exist as an abiding and universal phenomenon in a democracy.

But, then, .the overtones and political use of the term "minority" may be discarded.

Classification of Behaviour of Majority towards Minority

If we look at the attitudes of the majority towards the minority, we may be led to concur with Robert K. Merton's identification of four possible types of members of majority groups in terms of their attitudes and behaviour towards minorities.

Type 1

There are some 'all-weather liberals', who are unprejudiced towards minorities and avoid discrimination at all cost.

Type 2

There are some 'fair-weather liberals', who consider themselves unprejudiced but will 'bend with the wind' if it means some personal cost.

Type 3

There are some 'timid bigots' who hold prejudices against minorities, but because of legal pressure or financial interests, act in an egalitarian way.

Type 4

There are some 'active bigots' who hold strong prejudices against minority groups and practise discrimination against them.

Prejudice and Discrimination

The concept of minority is a recent development, while prejudice and antagonism have been widespread in human history.

To understand this, we need to look to psychology as well as sociology. We must distinguish between prejudice and discrimination.

Prejudice refers to opinions or attitudes held by members of one group about another; whereas discrimination refers to actual behaviour towards them. Prejudice involves holding preconceived views about an individual or group, often based upon hearsay rather than direct evidence; views which are resistant to change even in the face of new information. People may have favourable prejudices towards groups with which they identify and negative prejudices against others. Someone who is prejudiced against a particular grouping will refuse to give them 'a fair hearing'.

Discrimination refers to activities which serve to disqualify the members of one grouping from opportunities open to others—as when someone of Indian origin is refused a job made available to a white. Although prejudice is often the basis of discrimination, the two may exist separately. Prejudice operates mainly through the use of stereotypical thinking. In some circumstances, stereotypes are infused with attitudes of hostility or hatred towards some other group. This type of situation exists between a white and a black.

Somehow, one has to accept that this type of situation does not exist in India.

Historical Perspective

To clearly understand the concept of minority in present times, we must take a historical view. It is difficult to comprehend minority in the modern age without giving prime place to the impact of the expansion of the West over the past several centuries—especially the impact of Western colonization upon the rest of the world.

From the fifteenth century onwards the Europeans began to venture into uncharted seas and unexplored land masses, pursuing the aims of exploration and trade, but also conquering and subduing native peoples in many areas. Settling in these areas, they poured out in their millions from Europe. By way of the slave trade, they also brought about a large-scale movement of population from Africa to America.

From the seventeenth century to the present day, by an estimate, some 45 million people emigrated from Europe to the United States and Canada. Many went back to Europe again; but most settled permanently, and about 150 million people in North America today can trace their ancestry to this migration.

Similarly, some 50 million people in Central and South America are of European ancestry, mostly coming from Spain, Portugal and Italy.

Starting in the sixteenth century, about 10 million blacks were transported to the American continent.

In Africa and Australia, about 17 million people are of European ancestry, the majority are in South Africa colonized mainly by the British and the Dutch.

These population flows were the main basis of the ethnic composition of the United States, Canada, the countries of Central and South America, South Africa, Australia and New Zealand.

At the height of the colonial era, in the nineteenth and early twentieth centuries, Europeans also ruled over native populations throughout most of Africa, part of the Middle East, and in India, Burma and Malaya.

For most of the period of European expansion, ethnocentric attitudes were rife among the colonists, who believed themselves to be on a civilizing mission to the rest of the world.

The racist views separating whites from blacks became central to European attitudes.

Why did it happen? One reason is that an opposition between white and black as cultural symbols was deeply rooted in European culture. White had long been associated with purity, black with evil.

A second important factor influencing modern racism was simply the coinage and diffusion of the concept 'race' itself.

A third reason for the rise of modern racism lies in the exploitative relations which the Europeans established with non-white peoples.

Racism played an important part in the group closure whereby Europeans were the rulers, and non-whites the ruled.

Such is not the case with India. In India the British rule remained for about two centuries, and prior to that the Muslim rulers ruled in this country for seven to eight centuries. In fact, the British rulers took over from the Muslim rulers. During these periods, important ruling positions were held by the Muslims as well as the Hindus. Here, ethnicity and racism did not play that important part in the group closure. The situation started changing on the eve of independence, particularly, after the division of India.

With the adoption of the Constitution of India, equality became the watchword. Equality of opportunity in terms of educational development is the need of our people whether they belong to this group or that.

Why shouldn't there be a common school (as the public schools) for all boys whether of the majority or the minority group having uniform pattern of teaching and syllabus, with provisions for some periods in which classes in language, literature, culture of the minority groups may be held; and children may get the opportunity to benefit by these classes and learn about their own culture, tradition and language.

Instead of allowing the minority concept to be politicized, the minority groups could be made equal partners in the process of socio-economic, educational development. Given equal opportunity at the primary, secondary school levels, they will help themselves up and take advantage of the general, technical, professional education to find entry into the various positions in administration, academy, science and technology and professions.

Equality before law is of little use if discrimination persists in practice.

Speaking of the education in the U.S.A., schools in the North were not segregated in law but there had been pronounced segregation of blacks and whites because of different patterns of neighbourhood residence. Since blacks and whites live in largely separate neighbourhoods, their children attend different schools. Some affirmative actions were initiated to redress the balance where the minority groups were disfavoured. One example of such affirmative action is the transporting of children between school districts (taking children to schools outside their area in order to place white children in predominantly blacks schools, and the other way around) to achieve greater integration which began as a result of a Supreme Court decision that came into force in 1971.

The other forms of affirmative action tried out in the 1970s and 1980s in the USA include allocating a certain proportion of college places to minority groups in the knowledge that their grades might not match up to those of others. In order to break barriers similar steps could be devised in India to bring the very weak and neglected ones among the minorities and other groups into the mainstream of the national life. In this regard, the community action may also be initiated to open up educational institutions, and create proper conditions for providing quality education especially among the Muslim and the Buddhist minorities.

Immigration

In the post-Second World War period, Britain experienced immigration on an unprecedented scale. Most of the new residents came from the Commonwealth countries in response to job opportunities there. But the way the British reacted to this new influx of immigrants smelt of a class division.

However, those in governing circles were influenced by the notion of Britain's great imperial heritage, that West Indians, Indians, Pakistanis and Africans were all British subjects and entitled to settle in Britain. The notion of the governing elite did not change the attitude of the British towards the immigrants. Britain is now a multiracial nation; so is the USA.

India is from time immemorial a multilingual, multireligious nation. Some 11.4 per cent of the population is Muslim, 2.5 per cent of the population is Christian, 1.9 per cent of the population is Sikh, 0.71 per cent of the population is Buddhist and 0.1 per cent of the population is Parsi. They are the sons of the soil; and product of long cultural heritage of India which is based on tolerance and mutual respect. There is no deep-rooted source of prejudice and discrimination among them. Muslims, Christians, Buddhists, Parsis have lived together for centuries. Unlike the modern West, the minorities in India are not immigrants. In England, the sources of prejudice and discrimination are rather deep-rooted. Racism is, in some large degree, 'built into' broad social inequalities in the British society.

Often several West European countries have witnessed campaigns for returning migrants to their countries of origin, threats of deportation in the event of unemployment and other related policies. Such proposals become a disturbing threat to minority youth, often born in their host country, who would face the prospect of being forced to return to countries with which they have no real links. Ethnic discrimination persists in Western Europe. Racism is a daily reality to members of the new ethnic minorities throughout Western Europe today. Ethnic minorities are still perceived by many people as a threat; a threat to one's job, one's safety and the national culture. In most countries of the West, they face a future of continued discrimination, in a social climate characterized by anxiety and tension.

Such is not the case with the religious minorities in India; they have their own base and links rooted in the soil of India; they belong to India; India is their motherland.

However, over the last four decades or so, there are indications of increased social conflicts among religious communities. India's variegated social structure has several religious groups, and the tendency of violence is on an increase. Minority-majority relations are likely to worsen.

Majorities are becoming more self-aware; a sense of territorial nationalism is emerging both among majorities and selected minorities; international ties of some minorities are growing.

Geographical - Territorial - Demographic Interpretation

There are divergent views on the minority-majority question in India.

Myron Weiner quotes an Indian journalist who referred to India as a "Hindu island in an Islamic sea".

On the face of things it is widely understood that the Hindus are a majority. In fact, the Hindus also are a vast congeries of sub-caste minorities. Some of the religious groups who are treated as minorities constitute the actual majority in different geographical locations. In real terms, the minority-majority status has become a matter of self-ascription. It needs objective definition. What is a minority from one perspective is a majority from another.

Until the recent time, we did not look upon the Sikhs as a minority. Now, they are treated as a minority, and the Minorities

Commission of India included them in the list of minorities. If we look upon the Sikhs (with about 2.0%) in India's population, they are a minority. But, in Punjab, the Sikhs are a majority, and it is the Hindus who become a minority.

The Muslims with about 11.4% of India's population constitute India's largest religious minority; but in Jammu and Kashmir it is the Hindus who constitute a minority. Also in the districts of Malappuram in Kerala, Muslims constitute a majority.

Similarly, the Christians with approximately 2.5 per cent of India's population constitute a minority, but they constitute a majority in Nagaland.

It is very clear that India has such a medley of religious and linguistic groups that the sense of belonging to a minority depends upon where one lives; how much power and status one enjoys; and one's sense of community threat. There are people who consider the Hindus to be constituting the dominant core of Indian identity. They narrowly use the term 'minority' to refer to those who are not Hindus. In common parlance, they also equate the term "minority", with 'Muslims', as they form the largest body among the religious minorities in India. Even some of the schools and colleges have been seen as using the term 'minority school' or 'minority college'.

Besides the religious groups who regard themselves as India's minorities, there are caste, tribal and linguistic groups who are self-designated minorities, often dubbed as such.

The minority groups have a peculiar group identity; presume that they are socially and economically subordinate to others; or they believe that they suffer from discrimination, either from other groups in the society or from the state itself. To regard oneself as part of a minority in India is to suggest that one ought to take group action to remedy one's situation. To declare one's group a minority is a political act. In the Indian context, it is a way of calling attention to a situation of self-accepted deprivation.

The Minorities Commission of India listed the following groups in the category of religious minorities:

(i) The Muslims
(ii) The Christians
(iii) The Sikhs
(iv) The Buddhists

(v) The Parsis

A people who do not share what they regard as the central symbols of the society invariably view themselves as a minority. Symbol sharing is, perhaps, no less important than power sharing.

If we conceive of a minority as a category defined by the observed rather than by observers, a self-definition by a community itself, we are faced with a methodological problem of significant proportion. If we understand the term 'minority' as a socially negotiable concept, then, a community that regards itself and is regarded by others as a minority may under some circumstances cease to be a minority; while other communities may become minorities. In the United States, for example, Italian-Americans, Irish-Americans, Polish-Americans and Jews once regarded themselves as minorities, but now are seen as "ethnic"; while the term 'minority' has come to be reserved for those who are "disadvantaged". Who belongs to the category 'disadvantaged minority' as distinct from "ethnic" is politically and socially negotiable. In India, Sikhs are included as minorities; in West Bengal, Ramakrishna Mission schools are regarded as minority institutions; other communities may join them. In course of time, may be, some new minorities may assert claims; existing minorities may put forth new claims.

Then, we may commit the error of falling back upon the communities' self-perceptions regarding their minority status.

According to Myron Weiner, it is useful to think of four types of minorities in India:

Linguistic, religious, caste and tribal.

These can be further divided along three dimensions: whether minorities have a conception of a territorial homeland; the extent of the sense of cohesion within the community; and whether the community regards itself as a disadvantaged, or as an achieving minority. Also, the perceptions of other groups need to count to determine the minority status.

Linguistic Minorities

Each of India's States has an official language, those who speak another language as their mother tongue regard themselves as belonging to a linguistic minority.

The concerns of each of these linguistic minorities are quite different.

Urdu speakers have called for the establishment of Urdu as an official second language of the states in which they live. In fact, in some states, Urdu has been declared as an official second language.

There is a problem with the question of mother tongue in case of Muslim minority.

In Assam, the Muslim migrants from Bangladesh who report Assamese as their mother tongue are, in fact, Bengali speakers. They are not Urdu speakers. What would be the approach towards language in these cases?

In the coming decades, the demands of these groups, minorities and majorities are bound to force a rethinking of some of India's policies to manage conflict. Table 2.1 gives the decadal variation in population by religion between 1961 and 1991.

TABLE - 2.1
DECADAL VARIATION OF POPULATION BY RELIGION IN PERCENTAGE

Population by Religion	*1991*	*1981*	*1971*	*1961*
Buddhists	0.77	0.7	0.7	0.7
Christians	2.32	2.4	2.6	2.4
Muslims	11.67	11.4	11.2	10.7
(others which include Parsis)	0.43	0.4	0.4	0.3
Sikhs	1.99	2.0	1.9	1.8
Hindus	82.41	82.6	82.7	83.5

Source: India 1995, p. 19.

From the above table we can see that the population of the Buddhists has remained almost stable. The Christian population is slightly on decline. The Muslims have steadily increased from 10.7% of the total population in 1961 to 11.2% in 1971 to 11.4% in 1981 and to 11.6% in 1991. The increase in population among the Muslims is on account of two factors, i.e., natural growth of population, that is, increased birth rate; and immigration from neighbouring countries particularly, Bangladesh. The population of the Sikhs remains almost the same. There is a steady decline in the population of the Hindus, i.e., from 83.5% in 1961 to 82.7% in 1971 to 82.6% in 1981 and to 82.4% in 1991. This may be due to decline in the natural growth or fall in birth rate owing to the adoption of the family planning, or due to conversion into other religions.

The Muslims form a majority in Jammu and Kashmir. They constitute 21.3% of Kerala's population; 21.5% of West Bengal's population; 15.9% of Uttar Pradesh's population; 14.1% of Bihar's population and 11.0% of Karnataka's population. They are concentrated in selected districts of these states; and also are disproportionately urban. They constitute a majority in 9 districts; 30 to 50% of the population in 10 other districts; and 20 to 35% of the population in 20 more districts.

The Sikhs form a majority in Punjab constituting about 60.8% of the state's population. From 1961 to 1971 population of the Sikhs increased more rapidly in the state, and from 1971 to 1981 their growth continued to be higher. There has been a considerable amount of redesignation among the Sikhs who were previously Hindus.

The Sikhs are heavily urbanized, and are physically distinctive and noticeable minorities in cities. Myron Weiner called the Sikhs a diaspora community. About one-third of the Sikhs live in other parts of India outside Punjab.

The Christians forming about 2.32% of India's population are more numerous than the Sikhs, but less politically vocal than the Sikhs. Bulk of the Christians are in Kerala, Tamil Nadu, Andhra Pradesh; and are concentrated in Nagaland (80.2%) and Meghalaya (52.6%).

The Buddhists forming about 0.7% of India's population are closely associated with the Hindus as are the Jains.

The Bahais and the Jains are not included in this study.

Lack of Cohesion

Of the three major religious minorities, i.e., the Muslims, the Christians, and the Sikhs, none is cohesive. Among them the Sikhs are relatively more cohesive, yet, the Sikhs are divided between scheduled caste and non-scheduled caste Sikhs; Jat Sikhs and other high-caste Sikhs. The orthodox Sikhs even look askance at the heterodox Nirankaris.

The Christians lack the cohesion of the Sikhs; they are dispersed; speak the language of the region and are generally converts from tribes or low castes. The Christians of north-east are culturally distinct from Christians of South India — most of the north-east Christians are tribals.

The Muslims are even less cohesive. The Muslims of South-West India had long ties with the Arab world; they continue to migrate to the Gulf countries. In Kerala, they speak Malayalam; their diet and dress are close to the Hindus in the region.

Similarly, the Muslims in Kashmir have Kashmiri identity; by and large speak Kashmiri rather than Urdu. In West Bengal, majority of the Muslims speak Bengali; only a small percentage of Muslims speak Urdu. In Andhra Pradesh, the upper class Muslims (in Hyderabad region) formed the governing elite, and are, by and large, Urdu speaking.

Generally, north Indian Muslims had an association with the Muslim League, and participated in mainstream political parties. About 64% of the Muslims in the Hindi-speaking region speak Urdu. It is in this region that the Muslim League spread their influence and became the proponent of two-nation theory. Yet, the orthodox Muslims look down on the Ahmediyas, a heterodox sect, and treat them as non-Muslims.

Four major religions of India originated in this country (Hinduism, Buddhism, Jainism and Sikhism), and for the people of four other religions (Islam, Christianity, Zoroastrianism and Judaism) India is their motherland.

Article 25 of India's Constitution stipulates that the Sikhs, the Buddhists and the Jains cannot be excluded from the Hindu temples. The Hindus worship at Sikh gurdwaras, or at the tombs of saints, the Hindu families sometime declare some of their male children Sikhs and give them Sikh names. The Hindus incorporate tribal gods and worship a tribal deity. The tolerance for internal diversity and a readiness to incorporate others is not so well regarded by Islam, etc. The Sikhs and the Muslims consider politics and religion as inseparable.

Decadal increase in the population of the Muslims creates a sense of imbalance as shown in Table 2.1.

The common Muslims may not be in favour of the adoption

of family planning and limiting the size of the family because they are given to understand it as anti-Islamic.

There are some apparent religious differences between the Hindus and the Muslims. These differences are on idol worship, on monotheism and attitude towards the cow. They seemingly created a basic antipathy between the two communities which "helped to set them apart".

The Muslims of the Hindi-speaking areas, especially, Uttar Pradesh and Bihar, primed by these fundamental religious differences and already conscious of themselves as a separate religious community being aware that they are a minority, suspected that the Hindu majority would not only interfere with their religious practices, such as, cow sacrifice, but also would discriminate against them on such matters as 'education and employment'.

Here, the role of the political groups in influencing the ability of the elite to manipulate particular symbols is crucial.

They manipulate symbols of group identity for political purposes. The symbolic objective criteria on which the Hindu-Muslim relation generally centres are,

(i) Symbol of cow: The Hindu attitude towards cow protection; the Muslim attitude towards cow sacrifice;
(ii) Muslim personal law (Shariat) relating to marriage, divorce, and inheritance of property;
(iii) Attitude of the Hindus and the Muslims towards the Hindi and Urdu languages; to add further the mosque-temple issue is another element.

Each element of the traditional culture and its use by elites in politics is a crucial question.

Today the point is whether the elites are able to alter the definition of a group's boundary by manipulating sets of symbols.

Distinctive minority religious groups in present times have often developed into ethnically self-conscious communities; religious differences have been used or even created to establish between peoples barriers that have non-religious origins.

The Consociational Model

In plural societies in developing countries, such as, India, there may be an attempt to apply what Lijphart, a Dutch social scientist called the 'Consociational Model' to accommodate differences among the segmented religio-political groupings in the Dutch society.

Some of the characteristics of the consociational model, such as:

(i) overaching cooperation at the elite level in a culturally fragmented system;

(ii) some proportionality in recruitment to decision-making bodies, public services and in allocation of public funds; and

(iii) reasonable degree of autonomy for each segment to run its own internal affairs, may be applied to plural societies like India. Somehow this model needs to be worked out.

The idea behind working out this model is not to abolish or weaken the segmental divisions but to recognize them explicitly and turn the segments into constructive elements of strong and stable nation and democracy.

Defining Minority

In Social Science, in India, a question that has been generally evaded is: 'in what terms to define the 'minority'. Neither the Constitution of India, nor the judiciary which is the interpreter of the Constitution, has defined the minority in precise terms. The recent Bill on the (Statutory) Status of the Minorities Commission, also did not define minority.

The Constitution looks at the minority from two perspectives: (i) religious and (ii) linguistic.

The Minorities Commission deals mainly with the religious minorities, viz., the Muslims, the Christians, the Sikhs, the Buddhists, and the Parsis. The judiciary has hitherto viewed the minority in terms of population of a religious group in a state. Less than 50 per cent of a state's population which belongs to a religious community has been treated as a 'minority'. Truly speaking under Articles 29 and 30 of the Constitution of India, the term 'minority' has been given a wide connotation. Here, a minority is recognized as such on the basis of not only religion but also language, script or culture.

The majority-minority has been an issue before our nation since the dawn of independence. The British rulers posed themselves as the sole protector of the minorities in India. That led to the Hindu-Muslim divide and partition of the nation. The Muslim League stood up as the sole guarantor of the rights and safety of the Muslim minority.

The Government of 'Independent India' for the sake of a united, integrated nation, stood for the protection of the interests of the minorities in India.

Since then, the minority continued to remain a political question frequently raised and debated for political use.

Who are the minorities? What do they want? What is their need? The majority vis-a-vis the minority—these issues continued to bother the academics, the policy makers, and the political leaders of India.

Since the late sixties, the minority question became sharper and more glaring when Mrs Indira Gandhi set up a governmental machinery to look into the special problems of the minorities as a step towards promoting national integration. That the minorities mentioned by Mrs Gandhi implied the Muslims of India becomes more or less clear from her reference to Urdu, and particularly to her desire to see that the Urdu was assured its Constitutional guarantee. Since then, the minority question became more pronounced; minorities have been politically used, and their real problems of socio-economic, educational backwardness continued to persist.

Mrs Gandhi's attitude to Muslim demands, her inclination towards the Muslim communal organizations, her handling of Urdu aggrandizing demand, led to the minority being politically exploited.

The Muslim League always asserted that "it was the custodian of the interests of the Muslim minority in India". It is an irony that the Muslim League in Kerala passed a resolution demanding due recognition for Urdu even though the Kerala Muslims speak Malayalam.

Thus, the minority question became more crucial in India since 1967 general election and can be largely attributed to the propaganda carried out during the poll campaign (1967).[1]

1. G.S. Ghurye, 1974, *Whither India*, pp. 401-02, 407, Popular Prakashan, Mumbai.

The concept of minority in India continued to remain the game of power, played by the political parties/groups or State to reorient the belief and motivation of that particular group.

To define a minority as a social category, in a given society, who, because of their distinct physical or cultural characteristics, find themselves in situations of inequality within that society. A minority may be further defined as a group which is perceived as such by the other groups.

Minorities, as derived from the Constitution of India, include the Buddhists, the Christians, the Muslims, the Parsis, and the Sikhs, but, in common parlance, the term is generally understood to be equated with the Muslims. The Jains and the Bahais do not find any mention.

Minority in India has become a political term, with a political tinge; the minorities have been politically used, but their real problems of educational backwardness remain. The minorities have been used for the purpose of garnering votes after independence, but their socio-economic, educational problems have remained unattended.

The word minority as stated earlier has not been defined in the Constitution. The full Bench of the Kerala High Court 1964 (2) Ker. 478 (F.B.) held that as the word minority has not been defined in the Constitution, any community, religious or linguistic, which was numerically less than 50 per cent of the population of the state was a minority, and thus was entitled to the protection of Article 30. The Bench thus found that the Roman Catholics were a minority in Kerala.

Further the Apex Court summarized the effect of the decision in Sidharajbhai's case in the following propositions:

(i) "A school established by a minority-whether before or after the Constitution is within the ambit of Article 30(i), even though it imparts general education....";

(ii) The right guaranteed by Article 30(i) is a right that is absolute, and any law or executive direction which infringes the substance of that right is void to the extent of the infringement;

(iii) The absolute character of the right does not preclude regulations in the true interests of efficiency of instruction, discipline, health, sanitation, morality, public order and the like, as such regulations are not restrictions on the substance of the right guaranteed by the Constitution;

(iv) The fundamental right enshrined in Article 30(i) (Cultural and Educational Right) is intended to be effective and should not be whittled down by any regulative measure conceived in the interest, not of the minority educational institution, but of the public or the nation as a whole.

Religious Minority: Legal View

The Supreme Court held that though the Hindu community was a majority community in the whole of India, it was a minority community in Punjab, and the Arya Samajists though members of the Hindu community were a religious minority in Punjab.

Similarly, members of a Jain sect do form a minority in comparison to the total population of India as well as of West Bengal, and, according to the decision of the Supreme Court, in Kerala Education bill, 1957 (58) A. Sc. 956 the minority is to be determined by reference to the entire population of that state.

Here, the term "minority" is based on religion. For example, the Roman Catholics and Protestants profess the Christian religion, but it is indisputable that the Roman Catholics constitute a minority based on religion in Ulster where the Protestants constitute the majority; and conversely, the Protestants are a minority based on religion in Eire (Ireland) where Roman Catholics are in the majority.

Similarly, Shias and Sunnis profess the Islamic religion, but in Iran, for example, Sunnis are a minority based on religion. The provisions relating to the freedom of religion and protection of cultural and educational rights of religious minorities are designed to prevent discrimination, on the ground that the minorities profess a religion which is not that of the majority.

Further, it has been observed that it is not for a court to cut down fundamental rights because the court thinks that national interests require that the Hindu religion should not include minorities based on religion.

In effect, there are following points for consideration here:

(i) That under the provisions of the Constitution, the minorities have a right to establish and administer the educational institutions (Article 30); for the sake of preserving their customs, culture and language (Article 29).

(ii) That the minorities in question who find place in this study are the religious minorities, especially the Buddhists, the Christians, the Muslims, the Parsis, and the Sikhs;

(iii) That the other religious minority groups, like the Jains, the Bahais, the Arya Samajists, etc., have not been included in this study.

(iv) That the linguistic minorities who constitute the wider and larger groups are not included in the study.

(v) That the minorities have a right to establish and administer the educational institutions of their choice, but it is doubtful whether a right to establish and administer educational institution, does ensure a right to receive grants-in-aid or recognition with or without strings.

(vi) That the major grievances of the minority managed educational institutions lie in the area of grants-in-aid; and accord of recognition to the educational institutions established by them.

(vii) What use has the right to establish and administer the educational institutions without ensuring grants-in-aid; and due recognition of the institutions?

(viii) To make the educational institution effective and efficient, the grants-in-aid in various forms have to be ensured. Here, the responsibility and contribution of the state have to be larger and more positive.

(ix) At the same time, it has to be understood that there cannot be unfettered rights. Rights and obligations flow together. Grants-in-aid without accountability is an empty proposition. The observance of rules, regulations and statutory provisions from the government giving grants-in-aid will be an enabling clause for the sake of better academic performance, and for the health of the educational institutions. It is a mistake to treat it as an infringement on the rights of the minorities to establish and administer their educational institutions.

One point that arises here is who will look to the educational and cultural interests of the minorities?

Will it be the minority community itself, or its leaders?

Will it be any political party/group, such as, the Muslim League in case of the Muslims, or such other political party/group in case of other minority groups? The Muslim League often claims to be the custodian of the interests of the Muslim minority in India.

Will it be the Government in a professedly secular state like India?

The Constitution of India provides for the equality of all citizens. Therefore, the question of protection of the educational and cultural interests of any particular group of citizens seems anomalous.

The minority in India is a sociocultural, religious aggregate of groups often put to political use.

The Lahore Congress Session which was held in December (29-31), 1929, passed a resolution that "the Congress assures the Sikhs, the Muslims and other minorities that no solution thereof in any future Constitution will be acceptable to the Congress that does not give full satisfaction to the parties concerned".

Jawaharlal Nehru also admitted that the "communal forces exploiting the name of religion grew in strength and resulted in the partition of this country". Politics exploited religion, and religion used politics as its support base. The Muslim League became instrumental in creating a two-nation theory by using religion. India has been and is a land of many religions and races. Nehru also warned that the "forces of disruption — in India are — strong and we have to be vigilant".

He advised that in "politics we must not function" — as Hindus, Muslims, or Sikhs but as Indians. Here in India we have synthesized various forces and tried to reconcile them. The great beauty of our country is that we have such a "variety of cultures and religions". India has a variegated and yet essentially unified culture in which all have shared substantially.

However, the minorities in India are at varying levels. The case of Muslim and Sikh minorities is different from the Parsis, the Christians, and the Buddhists. The Muslim and the Sikh minorities are more vociferous, demanding, their voice is heard; the Parsis, the Christians and the Buddhists are more docile and less vociferous.

The Government of Pakistan is since its formation "meddling into the affairs of India especially relating to Muslim minority, as if, they are their concern" and not the concern of the Government of India. This irritated Mr Nehru and also created suspicion in the people's minds. Similarly, a recent resolution by Pakistan Legislature on Ram Janamabhumi-Babri Masjid issue raised the eyebrow of Government of India and the people. The cables sent to Liaquat Ali Khan on 24 August 1948, and 14 September 1948 by Nehru also refer to this situation. Recent nuclear experiment and growing insurgency across the Pakistan border continued to create suspicion in the minds of Indian Government and people.

The Britishers are gone, but the partition of India left a deep scar in people's memory.

Jawaharlal Nehru and Liaquat Ali Khan are gone, yet, the minority problem between Pakistan and India remains. Time has not been able to heal the wounds, and society has not been able to recover from its wounded feelings.

Minority-majority issue is often raised, and is subject to political exploitation. Why not change the terminology to change the people's mood and mind. Instead of majority and minority rights, the Constitution may be amended to have common rights of all citizens. Why a discriminated or a pampered category? This may be a right move towards a long-term solution to the problem.

Earlier, it was Hindus and Sikhs versus Muslims; then it became Hindus versus Sikhs; and the Hindus versus Muslims. The scene of these events largely remained limited to UP, Delhi, Punjab, Rajasthan and Bihar, what is called the Hindi heartland of Northern India which was largely affected by the partition.

Mutual suspicion is not the result of any alien influence, but is our own creation, and has bred the distrust which is behind all our troubles.

Pakistan is a state based on religion. How far it can remain free trying to influence politics is difficult to say.

The political masters in India often profess that no Indian should think of himself as a Hindu, a Muslim or of any religious entity so far as politics is concerned.

Our experience over these years shows that this has not happened. The religious entity of an average individual remains; and is aroused particularly because of some wrong steps in the past or present.

It has to be well understood that India has a variegated, and yet, essentially unified culture in which all have shared substantially. Jawaharlal Nehru (in his convocation address in Aligarh Muslim University in 1948) said:

"You are Muslims and I am a Hindu. We may adhere to any religious faith or even to none; but that does not take away from that cultural inheritance that is yours as well as mine. The past holds us together; why should the present or the future divide us in spirit?"

Selected Works of Jawaharlal Nehru, Second Series; 5, pp. 24-25.

People may have different faiths, beliefs, forms of worship, customs and manners, yet they may be held together by a common bond of cultural heritage which India acquired from antiquity. The irritants between the minority and majority may be dissolved by creating a bond of India's citizenship with common heritage to share, and equality of rights and opportunity to enjoy. The socio-economic, educational problems of the minorities must be meticulously attended to. Education is the key to social and economic progress. The national agenda of governance of the Bhartiya Janata Party-led government put special emphasis on socio-economic, educational development and opportunities of the minorities, particularly the Muslims.

THREE

Constitutional Provisions and Judicial Pronouncements on Educational Rights of the Minorities

In a pluralistic situation as ours, we cannot ignore the interests of the minorities and small communities.

It has been recognized that the safeguards for the minorities through Constitutional channel were the pre-independence development when the minorities, especially, the Muslims secured certain provisions at the time of more favourable climate, in which the liberal British policy towards the minorities and secular Congress views were so much helpful. The subcommittee on fundamental rights on the minorities submitted 'six main clauses' in 1947 for consideration by the Advisory Committee which ultimately submitted its recommendations to the Draft Committee of the Indian Constitution. Thus, after various deliberations and omissions, two Articles were provided finally in the Constitution for the interests of the minorities. They are Articles 29 and 30 which read as below:

> Article 29 (1): Any section of citizens residing in the territory of India or any part thereof having a distinct language, script or culture of its own shall have the right to conserve the same.
>
> Article 29 (2): No citizen shall be denied admission into any educational institution maintained by the state or receiving aid out of state funds on grounds only of religion, race, caste, language or any of them.
>
> Article 30 (1): All minorities, whether based on religion or language, shall have the right to establish and administer educational institutions of their choice.

> Article 30 (2): The state shall not, in granting aid to educational institutions, discriminate against any educational institution on the ground that it is under the management of a minority, whether based on religion or language.

These provisions of the Constitution resulted in wider interpretation and scope for never-ending legal battle in various courts in terms of every 'term' used in the Article 30 (1) and 30(2). The points of dispute include defining 'who is minority', 'minority character of the institution', 'right to administer', scope of state regulations, aim of establishing institutions, and regulations with regard to affiliation.

Minorities Based on Religion and Language

The Article 30(1) without leaving much scope for speculation sought to emphasize that claim to establishment and administration of an educational institution must be supported by an evidence that the institution in question was established by a minority distinguishable from others by the characteristics of either religion or language or both.

However, in order to decide which religious or linguistic group is a minority, the courts in their various disputes arrived at conclusions in different ways. In Kerala Education Bill, the Supreme Court suggesting the technique of arithmetical tabulation, held that a minority means a "community which is numerically less than 50 per cent" of the total population of the state (AIR 1985 SC 956). Nevertheless, in this case, the court did not make it clear while calculating the percentage of the minority population which should be taken as one single unit whether the whole of India, or a state in which the institution is situated, or, a district. This question was finally resolved in D.A.V. College, Jullundhar vs State of Punjab case, in which the Supreme Court held that unit is to be determined only in relation to the particular legislature, namely, that if it is the State Legislature, the minorities have to be determined in relation to the population of the state.

Objective of Establishment of Minority Institution

The idea of giving special rights to the minorities is not to have a kind of privileged or pampered section of the population but to give to the minorities a sense of security and a feeling of confidence (Justice Khanna: AIR 1974 SC 1389).

Delineating the scope of Article 30(1) in Kerala Education Bill, Justice S.R. Das held that "what the Article says and means is that the religious and the linguistic minorities should have the right to establish educational institutions of their choice. There is no limitation placed on the subjects to be taught in such educational institutions. As such, minorities will ordinarily desire that their children should be brought up properly and efficiently, and be eligible for higher university education, and go out in the world fully equipped with such intellectual qualities as will make them fit; educational institutions of their choice will necessarily include institutions imparting general secular education also. In other words, the Article leaves it to their choice to establish such educational institutions as will serve both purposes, namely, the purpose of conserving their religion, language, or culture, and also the purpose of giving a thorough good general education to their children (AIR 1958 SC 956).

Right to Establish and Administer

The right to 'establish and administer the educational institutions of their choice' is available to minorities only when the proof of establishment is supplied beyond doubt and when claims are disputed in the court. A review of various judgements shows that while determining the status of establishment, the courts have taken into consideration the important factors, such as, name of the institution, persons involved in the establishment, sources of funds; subjection to legal provisions and expression of intention. However, the courts have attached importance to different factors at different times by placing wider discretion in one or other factor. (AIR 1970 SC 2079, AIR 1975 SC 1821, AIR 1974 SC 1389, AIR 1971 SC 1739, AIR 190 SC 259, AIR 1970 SC 2079, AIR 1974...197, AIR 1958 Put 389, AIR 19636 Put 54).

However, the various judgements stressed that the minorities secured two rights under Article 30(1) (i.e.) (i) to establish and (ii) to administer, and have affirmed in several cases that the minority will have the right to administer educational institutions of their choice provided they have established them. The words 'establish' and 'administer' in the Article must be read conjunctively, and so read, it gives the right to the minorities to administer an educational institution provided it has been established by it. (I.C.S.R. 1968 846-47, AIR 1976 Patna 83, AIR 1975 Kerala 87, AIR 1973 Patna 01, AIR 1951 Assam 163, AIR 1982 Andhra 64)

In effect, "Article 30 is a charter of educational rights. It guarantees, in absolute terms, the right of linguistic and religious minorities to establish and administer educational institutions of their choice and, at the same time, claim grants-in-aid without any discrimination based upon religion or language. The fact that the Constitution does not impose any express restriction in the scope of the enjoyment of this right, ... shows that the frames intended to make its scope unfettered. This does not, however, mean that the state cannot impose reasonable restrictions of a regulatory character for maintaining standards of education. This point has been made abundantly clear in judicial pronouncements".

The Supreme Court on the Kerala Educational Bill (1957) had observed, "it is however well-known that in modern times, the demands and necessities of modern educational institutions to be properly and efficiently run require considerable expense which cannot be met fully by fees collected from scholars and private endowments which are not adequate, and therefore, no educational institution can be maintained in a state of efficiency and usefulness without substantial aid from the state".

The same position has been reiterated by the Supreme Court in the case of Sidhrajbhai:

Again in the circumstances prevailing in the country, no educational institution could, in actual practice, be maintained without aid from the state, and if it could not get it unless it surrendered its rights, it would, because of financial necessities, be compelled to give up its rights under Article 30(1).

The observations of the Supreme Court made in the context of rights of minorities under Article 30, however apply *mutatis mutandis* to all educational institutions whose rights are infringed.

Autonomy of the Administration of Educational Institution

Administration means 'management of the affairs' of the institution. The management must be free of control so that the founders or their nominees could run the institution according to their way of thinking. The law which interferes with the composition of the managing committee as constituted by the minority is an abridgement of the right of the religious minorities to administer the educational institutions established by them (1971 SCR 734, AIR 1970 SC 2079, AIR 1969 SC 465).

The right of administration of minority institutions cannot be restricted in the matter of appointment of a principal and disciplinary action against a teaching staff. The right to appoint a principal cannot by state be given to a committee with the vice-chancellor's nominee, where the institution is a minority institution.

If a minority institution terminates the services of a teacher after proper enquiry against him/her an appeal against that decision to the vice-chancellor cannot be provided for, by state. Such a power would be a grave encroachment on the right of the institution to enforce and ensure discipline and a blanket power given to an outsider would not be valid (GOI 1987:33).

However, the judicial views of right to administer sought to bring a balance between preserving the Article 30(1) and to maintain the standard of education in such institutions. As a matter of fact, the right to administer educational institution does not mean the right to maladminister. The State may prescribe reasonable regulations to ensure the excellence of minority institutions. However, government's attempt to take over a minority institution (even for a limited period) is a violation of the right to manage and administer an educational institution (1959 SCR 955: (AIR 1958 SC 996).

The meaning of Article 30(1) implies that the right to establish and administer a minority institution cannot be interfered with. However, the restrictions by way of regulations for the purpose of maintaining the educational standards of the institutions can be validly imposed. For maintaining the educational standards of the institution as a whole, it is necessary to ensure that it is properly staffed. The conditions imposing the minimum qualifications of staff, their pay, and other benefits, their service conditions, the imposition of punishment will all be covered, and regulations of such a nature have been held to be valid. In the case of institutions that received aid, it is the duty of the government who grants aid to see that well qualified persons are selected, their pay and other emoluments are guaranteed and service conditions secured. So far as the institutions receiving aid are concerned, if the regulations are made for the purpose of safeguarding the rights of the staff the validity cannot be questioned as long as the regulations do not discriminate minority institution on the ground of religion or language.

The right guaranteed to religious and linguistic minorities by Article 30(1) is twofold, to establish and administer educational institutions of "their own choice". These words indicate that the extent of the right is to be determined not with reference to any concept of state necessity and general societal interest but with reference to the educational institutions themselves, i.e., to the goal of making educational institution an effective vehicle of education for minority community or other persons who resort to it.

Recognition and Affiliation

The right to recognition and affiliation is not expressly recognized by Article 30(1). The courts are conscious that in the absence of such a right the options otherwise open to minority institutions may not be such as to enable them to effectively exercise their rights under Article 30(1). The courts had ruled that the state cannot take away the right provided in Article 30(1) by employing indirect methods, such as, imposing regulatory conditions so as to adversely affect the minority character of the institution (AIR 1958 SC 956, AIR 1958 SC 985, AIR 1974 SC 1989).

A minority institution has no fundamental right to be affiliated to a university. However, the refusal of affiliation unless certain terms and conditions are satisfied by the minority would be unconstitutional if the terms and conditions are such as to deny progress and autonomy of the institution. Such a denial would be in violation of the provisions of Article 30. The State or university may prescribe a course of study as a condition of affiliation, but not so as to take away the freedom of management of administration, or so as to reduce the institution to a mere satellite of the university or the state, or to annihilate the personality of the institution.

Medium of Instruction

Minority institutions cannot be required to affiliate themselves compulsorily to a university which prescribes as the sole and exclusive medium of instruction, a language which is not the language of the minority. No inconvenience or difficulties, administrative or financial can justify the infringement of the guaranteed rights (AIR 1974 SC 1389).

Regulatory Provisions

A recent judgement of the Supreme Court clarifies certain areas of the applicability of Article 30 of the Constitution to minority institutions. The court held that by virtue of Article 30(1), two rights are guaranteed to religious and linguistic minorities, namely, right to establish and right to administer educational institutions of their own choice. The extent of right is to be determined not with reference to any concept of necessity of general social interest, but with reference to the educational institutions themselves, that is, to say with reference to the goal of making the institutions "effective vehicles of education for the minority community or other persons who resort to them". Regulatory measures designed to achieve the above object do not impinge upon the right guaranteed by Article 30(1).

The Supreme Court ruled that the government aided minority educational institutions are entitled to prefer candidates of their own community for admissions with a view to maintain their minority character, subject to conformity with their university standards.

The State may regulate the intake in this category with regard to the need of the community in the area which the institution is going to serve. But in no case, shall such an intake exceed 50 per cent of annual admission. The minority institutions shall make available at least 50 per cent of the annual admission to members of communities other than the minority community. The admission of other community candidates shall be done purely on the basis of merit (*Times of India*, 7.12.1991).

Amendment to Legislation in State

The Tamil Nadu State Assembly in its budget session (1992) made amendments to the Tamil Nadu Recognised Private Schools

(Regulation) Act 1973 and the Tamil Nadu Private Colleges (Regulation) Act 1976 in order to give the government more powers to regulate the affairs of the minority institutions. The reaction to this measure was as follows:

Complaints from teachers of several minorities run schools and colleges, arbitrary appointments and dismissals besides alleged irregularities in payment of salaries. The case, in instance, is the Madras Christian College in which three teachers were sacked.

Amendment Provisions

The provision of the amendments sought to:

(i) Bar the managements of private institutions from suspending or dismissing a student or a teacher without reference to a competent government authority.

(ii) Registration of Managing Committee with the Government; and

(iii) Periodic inspection by a State agency.

Changes in States

Between 1978 and 1985 nine states (including Karnataka, Andhra Pradesh, West Bengal, and Bihar) sought to increase government control over minority institutions by amending their education Acts.

The attempts to control over minority institutions also included: attempts to (i) derecognize private schools; and

(ii) impose a surcharge on the 'surplus' income of minority and charitable institutions.

In two cases — Karnataka and Kerala — certain measures regarded as an attack on the rights of minority institutions were later dropped following protests.

The Tamil Nadu Government's attempt to regulate the functioning of minority educational institutions in the state had been severely resented by a section of the minority, especially, the Christian community.

The Muslims were also opposed to state interference in minority institutions. The Sikhs too are in the same mood considering the attempt to regulate the functioning of minority institutions as an attack on minority rights.

The representatives of various minority organizations argue that the Constitution recognizes the right of religious minorities to run their own educational establishments, and there is no reason why the government should interfere in their affairs.

They also admit that there are 'black sheep' — institutions where managements are arbitrary — but the point is 'does this make the entire system sick?'

By an estimate, there are about 80,000 schools and colleges run by various denominations—national bodies—Christians, Muslims, and Sikhs; — it is possible that a few are not being run properly.

They claim that the majority of them are above board, and they attempt to "punish" them on account of a few "deviants"; would demoralize them and could affect their performance. "It would be absurd to generalize on the basis of a few stray cases and tar all minority institutions with the same brush", is the view of some Muslim intellectuals. Most of the bodies which run these institutions have their own regulatory mechanism, they claim.

Some representative members of minorities emphasize a point, time and again, that they are not averse to state intervention if it is limited to ensuring that managements do not abuse their powers. At the same time, they say that such intervention almost invariably assumes the form of interference. "We have seen that willy nilly the idea is to dilute the autonomy of such institutions and it is this that we don't want", said the President of the Organisation of Christians in India (OCI claim to have a membership of about 20,000).

The representatives of some political parties (like CPI and CPM) acknowledge the constitutional position in minority institutions, and stress the need to uphold it, but point out that this should not be turned into a licence. "There must be safeguards to ensure that the interests of the staff and students are not compromised". They hold that the government safeguards do not necessarily mean interference in the affairs of an institution.

The Centre has also laid down some guidelines with regard to the administration of minority institutions. Since education is a state subject, the Centre has a limited role and it expects the State Governments to uphold the Constitutional position, is the view of some officials of the University Grants Commission.

Whether the institutions funded by the Government cannot claim total "immunity". The college affiliated to State or Central universities and financed by government to the tune of about 90 per cent must be held accountable. The institutions run entirely with private resources like the various public schools may have a case when they insist on complete autonomy. But "these minority institutions expose themselves to the charge of eating their cake and having it too" — a luxury indeed in these difficult days, is the comment of a national press.

Some of the salient points of the various pronouncements of the Supreme Court of India,[1] and some High Courts are indicated here:

(i) A minority institution seeking aid and recognition must be subject to regulatory provisions which are reasonable and consistent with Article 30(1) of the Constitution of India.[1]

(ii) A minority institution which, does not seek aid or recognition from the state or the Education Board need not be subject to regulatory provisions.

(iii) The minority institution cannot be allowed to fall below the standard of excellence expected of educational institutions or under the guise of exclusive right of management to decline to follow the general pattern.

(iv) The minority institution has a right to enforce and ensure discipline in its administrative affairs.

(v) The management of a minority educational institution cannot be permitted under the guise of the fundamental right guaranteed by Article 30(1) of the Constitution to oppress or exploit its employees.

(vi) It is open to the state to prescribe condition for granting recognition or disbursing aid.

1. A.K. Shah, 1991, Education and Educational Institutions Cases 1950-91, p. 14, Allahabad: Malhotra Law House.

FOUR

An Analysis of the Minority Managed Educational Institutions

The analysis of the minority managed educational institutions gives us the following details:

1. Institutional Data Schedule
2. Percentage distribution of institutions
3. Aided and unaided institutions
4. Time Gap between Recognition and Establishment
5. Teaching Staff from the Minority Community
6. Teacher-Student Ratio
7. Infrastructural Facilities Available

Institutional Data Schedule

TABLE - 4.1
PERCENTAGE DISTRIBUTION OF BREAK-UP OF INSTITUTIONS STUDIED IN DIFFERENT CATEGORIES

Type of Institution	*Mus-lim (%)*	*Chris-tian (%)*	*Sikhs (%)*	*Parsi (%)*	*Buddh-ists (%)*	*Total of all Types of Institutions*
1. Primary	18	7	-	9	17	70
2. Upper Primary	5	7	-	-	17	25
3. Secondary	22	14	14	82	50	150
4. Higher Secondary	29	36	14	-	-	125
5. Pre-University/ Inter College	5	-	7	-	-	20
6. Graduate	11	7	43	9	16	80
7. Postgraduate	8	29	22	-	-	60
8. Professional/ Technical	2	-	-	-	-	5
Total	100	100	100	100	100	535

The two studies on "Financial and Non-Financial Grievances of the Minority Managed Educational Institutions in India", which were conducted simultaneously, collected 535 samples of Institution Data schedules in all, in common.

Out of total samples of 535, about 58% are Muslim institutions of different types, 13% each from Christian and Sikh institutions, 10% of them are Parsi and 6% of them are Buddhist institutions of various types.

Out of 310 Muslim institutions, less than one-fifth of them are primary schools, 5 per cent are upper primary, slightly above one-fifth are secondary schools, less than three-tenths are higher secondary and one-tenth of them are graduate colleges. The samples consisted of postgraduates, professional and technical institutions too.

More than one-third of samples of 70 Christian institutions are higher secondary with another less than three-tenths being postgraduate institutes.

7% samples each were derived from primary, upper primary schools and graduate college, while 14% of samples of Christian institutions are secondary schools.

70 samples to represent 'Sikh institutions' were derived from more than six-tenths of graduate and postgraduate colleges and less than three-tenths from secondary and higher secondary schools while just 7% from inter colleges.

55 samples of Parsi institutions consisted of more than eight-tenths from secondary schools with rest of them derived in equal proportions from primary schools and graduate colleges.

Half of the 30 Buddhist samples are from secondary schools while the rest are derived in equal proportions from primary and upper primary schools and graduate colleges.

Table 4.2 shows the break-up of institutions according to whether government aid is received or not at the institution.

Nearly seven-tenths of the Muslim institutions studied are aided while eight-tenths of the Christian institutions are aided.

More than seven-tenths of the Sikh and Buddhist institutions are aided while all the Buddhists institutions studied receive grants-in-aid of some kind or other.

Keeping in view the nature or objective of the study, major

emphasis is to be given to aided institutions, and thereby, majority of the samples derived are from this category. However, in order to have a comprehensive understanding of the problem considerable number of unaided institutions were also included.

TABLE - 4.2
PERCENTAGE DISTRIBUTION OF AIDED OR UNAIDED INSTITUTIONS INCLUDED IN THE STUDY

Educational Institutions	*Aided (%)*	*Unaided (%)*	*No. Data (%)*	*Total (%)*	*Total No. of Question-naires*
1	2	3	4	5	6
1. Muslim	68	31	1	100	310
2. Christian	79	21	-	100	70
3. Sikh	72	14	14	100	70
4. Parsi	73	27	-	100	55
5. Buddhist	100	-	-	100	30

Table 4.3 gives us the time taken for recognition from the year of establishment. A cursory look at this table reveals that more than half of the minority institutions received recognition within a year of establishment. To be more specific, more than half of the Muslim managed institutions, six-tenths of Sikh and Christian institutions, less than half of Parsi, and more than six-tenths of Buddhist institutions, altogether 56 per cent of all minority managed institutions had been recognized by the concerned authorities within a year of their establishment. Another, one-tenth of all institutions took about one year to get recognition while more than one-tenth of Muslim, Sikh and near about three-tenths of Parsi institutions took anything between two or five years to obtain recognition.

Another three-tenths of Christian institutions took between six to ten years to get recognition. A special case of more than one-tenth of Muslim institutions, and near about one-tenth of Parsi institutions which took more than 10 years to get recognized, was also there.

From this table, while it becomes evident that majority of the institutions set up by the minority community face no difficulty from the authorities who duly accorded recognition within reasonable period; it is not to be overlooked that a considerable proportion, however may it be statistically insignificant, were recognized by authorities after long period of wait from the year of establishment. However, this is not to be inferred from this table as this conceals the information on what was the period that elapsed between the initial application for recognition and the year of establishment. Generally the institutions are very eager to get recognition and the first thing they do after establishing the institution is to get the same recognised.

TABLE - 4.3
PERCENTAGE DISTRIBUTION OF INSTITUTIONS IN 'TIME-GAP' BETWEEN YEAR OF ESTABLISHMENT OF INSTITUTIONS AND YEAR OF RECOGNITION OF THE INSTITUTIONS

Time-Gap	*Muslim (%)*	*Christian (%)*	*Sikhs (%)*	*Parsi (%)*	*Buddhists (%)*	*Total No. of Question-naires*
1	2	3	4	5	6	7
1. Same year	55	64	57	45	66	300
2. 1 year only	6	-	29	9	17	50
3. 2-5 years	13	7	14	28	-	70
4. 6-10 years	6	29	-	-	17	45
5. More than 10 years	13	-	-	9	-	45
6. No data	7	-	-	9	-	25
Total	100	100	100	100	100	535

During our field investigations, two sides of the picture emerged each from institution and concerned authorities, while management reported of harassment by the government authorities who in turn accuse the institution of not following the rules and norms for according recognition. This point merits particular attention.

Table 4.4 gives us the percentage distribution of teaching staff belonging to minority community. In a total of 535 institutions studied, there were just 15 institutions all of which were Buddhist institutions which have less than 10% as members of the teaching staff from minority community. In other words, half of the Buddhist institutions have appointed minority community members in less than 10% of the entire teaching staff and in another half of the Buddhist institutions the minority community forms between 25-50 per cent of the teaching staff.

TABLE - 4.4
PERCENTAGE DISTRIBUTION OF TEACHING STAFF THAT BELONGS TO MINORITY COMMUNITY

Percentage of Teaching Staff that belongs to Minority Community	*No. of Institutions in the Distribution*					
	Muslim	*Christian*	*Sikhs*	*Parsi*	*Buddhists*	*Total No. of Institutions*
Below 10%	Nil	Nil	Nil	Nil	15	15
10-25%	5	Nil	5	15	Nil	25
25-50%	20	10	15	40	15	100
50-90%	110	45	25	Nil	Nil	180
90-100%	175	15	25	Nil	Nil	215
Total	310	70	70	55	30	535

In more than one-fourth of Parsi institutions, 10-25 per cent of teaching staff belong to minority community while in another three-fourths, 25-50 per cent of teaching staff are minority community people.

Less than one-third of the Sikh institutions have anything between 90-100 per cent of their teaching staff who belong to minority community and in another equal proportion of Sikh institutions, 50-90 per cent of the teaching staff are from the minority community. More than one-fourth of Sikh institutions employed 25-50 per cent of the teaching staff are from minority community.

In about six-tenths of Christian institutions 50-90 per cent of teaching staff are from the minority community. Another one-fifth of institutions have 90-100 per cent of the teaching staff are from the minority community.

In six-tenths of Muslim institutions 90-100 per cent of teaching staff are from the minority community; and in another one-third of Muslim institutions 50-90 per cent of the staff are from the minority community. In one-fourth of Muslim institutions 25-50 per cent of the teaching staff represent the minority community.

It is to be noted that though the term minority community is used here to represent all five religious minority communities; as far as most of the Muslim institutions are concerned, they are all Muslim teaching staff institutions.

Table 4.5 shows the percentage of various types of institutions managed by minority communities in different student-teacher ratios. The table shows that all professional, technical institutions and inter colleges have anything between 1-30 students only per teacher.

TABLE - 4.5
PERCENTAGE DISTRIBUTION OF INSTITUTIONS ACCORDING TO TEACHER-STUDENT RATIO

Type of Institution	*Number of Students per Teacher*				
	1-30 (%)	*30-60 (%)*	*60-100 (%)*	*Above 100 (%)*	*Total (%)*
Primary	57	36	7	-	100
Upper Primary	80	20	-	-	100
Secondary	61	33	3	3	100
Higher Secondary	40	60	-	-	100
Pre-Univ./Inter College	100	-	-	-	100
Graduate	63	37	-	-	100
Postgraduate	58	42	-	-	100
Professional/Technical	100	-	-	-	100
Total Questionnaires	310	210	10	5	535

Another eight-tenths of upper primary, six-tenths of secondary and primary, postgraduate and graduate colleges are also in the same category. Only about four-tenths of higher secondary institutions belong to this category.

Six-tenths of higher secondary schools of all minority managed institutions and one-third of secondary schools, near about four-tenths of primary, graduate and postgraduate colleges have students ranging between 30-60 per teacher. Thus, about four-tenths of all types of institutions are in this category which underlines the overburden to the teachers at these institutions.

Table 4.6 gives the percentage distribution of institutions having minimum facilities. In Andhra Pradesh, all the educational institutions have electricity, toilet; while library and audio-visual aids are available in eight-tenths of the institutions, laboratory in six-tenths, and playground only in four-tenths of the institutions.

Medical and computer facilities find no place in any of the institutions. Details regarding other infrastructure related to educational institutions like distance from bus stand, railway station, post and telegraph offices and particulars about co-curricular activities have been given in Tables 4.7 to 4.10.

The four-tenths of institutions in Andhra Pradesh are situated at less than half kilometer from the bus stand, while similar proportion of institutions are in between 1/2-2 km. away from the bus stand. About one-fifth of institutions are 5 km away from the bus stand. About eight-tenths of these institutions however, have railway station within 3 km. The post office and telegraph office are available to all the institutions in Andhra Pradesh within 5 kms; and phone facility within 3 kms. None of the institutions have any co-curricular activities, such as National Service Scheme (NSS), National Cadet Corps. (NCC) and adult education programmes.

In Bihar, Chandigarh and Haryana all the minority institutions have electricity, toilet, library, laboratory, audio-visual aids and playground. In Bihar and Haryana all the institutions are situated between 1/2 to 2 km. from the bus stand; and 3 km. from the railway station. They have post office and telephone facility within the premises and telegraph office within 5 km. In Chandigarh, two-thirds of institutions are less than 1/2 km from bus stand and between 3 to 10 km from railway station.

All the institutions in Delhi, Gujarat, Punjab, Tamil Nadu and West Bengal have electricity and toilet facilities. While majority of the institutions in these states have library, laboratory, audio-visual aids, playground with an exception of two-thirds of institutions in Gujarat; more than half of the institutions in Punjab and Tamil Nadu do not have laboratory.

This general trend is exhibited in similar fashion in case of majority of institutions in various states; whereas the notable features are that one-fifth of institutions in Kerala, one-tenth of institutions in Maharashtra, one-fourth in Mizoram, and one-third in Orissa do not have electricity at the institution. A much lesser proportion of these institutions lack other facilities like toilet, library, laboratory, audio-visual aids. The majority of the institutions in various states do not have computer and medical facilities.

TABLE - 4.6

PERCENTAGE DISTRIBUTION OF INSTITUTIONS HAVING MINIMUM FACILITIES AT THE INSTITUTION

	State	*Electricity* (%)	*Toilet* (%)	*Library* (%)	*Laboratory* (%)	*Audio-visual Aids* (%)	*Play-ground* (%)	*Medical* (%)	*Computer* (%)	*Total No. of Institutions Studied*
1.	Andhra Pradesh	100	100	80	60	80	40	0	0	25
2.	Bihar	100	100	100	0	100	100	0	0	5
3.	Chandigarh	100	100	100	100	100	100	0	0	15
4.	Delhi	100	100	100	75	100	75	0	0	20
5.	Gujarat	100	100	83	33	83	100	33	0	30
6.	Haryana	100	100	100	0	100	100	100	0	5
7.	Karnataka	100	95	100	20	45	90	50	65	100
8.	Kerala	78	89	100	89	78	100	22	22	45
9.	Maharashtra	88	94	82	18	76	76	54	35	85
10.	Mizoram	75	50	50	0	50	100	0	0	20
11.	Orissa	67	100	100	67	67	100	67	0	15
12.	Punjab	100	100	100	44	100	78	89	100	45
13.	Tamil Nadu	100	100	91	45	73	100	64	45	55
14.	Uttar Pradesh	100	92	83	50	33	75	25	20	60
15.	West Bengal	100	100	0	0	0	0	50	0	10
	All India	-	-	-		-	-	-	-	535

Note: Figures relate to the per cent of institutions having each facility separately out of total number of institutions studied.

TABLE - 4.7
PERCENTAGE DISTRIBUTION OF INSTITUTIONS ACCORDING TO DISTANCE OF THE INSTITUTION FROM BUS-STAND

	State	*Less than 1/2 km (%)*	*1/2-2 km (%)*	*2-5 km (%)*	*More than 5 km (%)*	*Total No. of Questionnaires*
1.	Andhra Pradesh	40	40	Nil	20	25
2.	Bihar	-	100	-	-	5
3.	Chandigarh	67	Nil	33	-	15
4.	Delhi	75	25	-	-	20
5.	Gujarat	33	67	-	-	30
6.	Haryana	-	100	-	-	5
7.	Karnataka	30	50	15	5	100
8.	Kerala	11	33	33	23	45
9.	Maharashtra	47	47	6	-	85
10.	Mizoram	25	75	-	-	20
11.	Orissa	33	67	-	-	15
12.	Punjab	-	56	33	11	45
13.	Tamil Nadu	36	64	-	-	55
14.	Uttar Pradesh	58	25	8	9	60
15.	West Bengal	-	100	-	-	10
						535

TABLE - 4.8
PERCENTAGE DISTRIBUTION OF INSTITUTIONS ACCORDING TO THE DISTANCE OF THE INSTITUTION FROM RAILWAY STATION

	State/U.T.	*Up to 3 km %*	*3-10 km %*	*10-30 km %*	*30-50 km %*	*Above 50 km %*	*Total Questionnaires Studied*
1.	Andhra Pradesh	80	Nil	20	Nil	Nil	25
2.	Bihar	100	-	-	-	-	25
3.	Chandigarh	33	67	-	-	-	15
4.	Delhi	100	-	-	-	-	20
5.	Gujarat	83	17	-	-	-	30
6.	Haryana	100	-	-	-	-	5
7.	Karnataka	50	50	-	-	-	100
8.	Kerala	0	44	66	-	-	45
9.	Maharashtra	71	12	-	17	-	85
10.	Mizoram	Nil	-	-	-	100	20
11.	Orissa	Nil	-	-	-	100	15
12.	Punjab	56	44	-	-	-	45
13.	Tamil Nadu	82	18	-	-	-	55
14.	Uttar Pradesh	58	25	8	-	9	60
15.	West Bengal	100	-	-	-	-	10

Note: Percentages are individual for every state and total number of institutions studied in every state form 100 per cent.

TABLE - 4.9

PERCENTAGE DISTRIBUTION OF INSTITUTIONS ACCORDING TO THE DISTANCE OF THE INSTITUTIONS FROM THE FOLLOWING INFRASTRUCTURE FACILITIES

		Post Office				Telegraph		Telephone				Total No. of
	State/U.T.	Up to 1 km	1-5 km	5-10 km	Above 10 km	Up to 5 km	Above 5 km	Within Premises	Up to 3 km	3-5 km	Above 5 km	Question-naires studied
1.	Andhra Pradesh	60	40	-	-	100	-	40	60	-	-	25
2.	Bihar	100	-	-	-	100	-	100	-	-	-	5
3.	Chandigarh	100	-	-	-	100	-	100	-	-	-	15
4.	Delhi	75	25	-	-	100	-	100	-	-	-	20
5.	Gujarat	50	50	-	-	100	-	83	17	-	-	30
6.	Haryana	100	-	-	-	100	-	100	-	-	-	5
7.	Karnataka	60	30	10	-	90	10	45	40	10	5	100
8.	Kerala	56	33	11	-	89	11	56	44	-	-	45
9.	Maharashtra	88	12	-	-	100	-	88	12	-	-	85
10.	Mizoram	50	50	-	-	50	50	58	12	-	-	20
11.	Orissa	67	33	-	-	100	-	-	100	-	-	15
12.	Punjab	56	44	-	-	100	-	89	11	-	-	45
13.	Tamil Nadu	73	27	-	-	100	-	91	19	-	-	55
14.	Uttar Pradesh	75	25	-	-	75	25	67	-	23	-	60
15.	West Bengal	100	-	-	-	100	-	-	100	-	-	10
												535

TABLE - 4.10
PERCENTAGE DISTRIBUTION OF INSTITUTIONS REPORTED HAVING FOLLOWING CO-CURRICULAR ACTIVITIES

	State/U.T.	*N.S.S.*	*Adult Education*	*N.C.C.*
1.	Andhra Pradesh	Nil	Nil	Nil
2.	Bihar	Nil	Nil	Nil
3.	Chandigarh	67	100	67
4.	Delhi	25	Nil	Nil
5.	Gujarat	Nil	50	Nil
6.	Haryana	100	100	100
7.	Karnataka	5	20	10
8.	Kerala	44	11	44
9.	Maharashtra	6	67	22
10.	Mizoram	25	25	Nil
11.	Orissa	Nil	67	Nil
12.	Punjab	89	78	89
13.	Tamil Nadu	36	27	36
14.	Uttar Pradesh	8	33	33
15.	West Bengal	Nil	100	Nil

The majority of these institutions also have bus stand and railway station within easy reach with exception of Mizoram and Orissa where all institutions studied are more than 50 km away from railway station. Again post office, telegraph and phone facilities are within the reach, while some proportions of these institutions have these facilities at longer distances than desirable.

As far as the co-curricular activities are concerned, the only uniform pattern is that the great majority of the institutions do not have these programmes with exceptions in a few states.

It should be noted that over a period of time the intake of students at the institutions is ever on the increase only reflecting the population pressure in India, while recruitment of teachers is on the decrease at an individual institution duly reflects upon the process of economic development. This picture generally, is also applicable to other non-minority institutions. Further, point raised at these institutions for unpleasant student-ratio, is the restriction by the government authorities on recruitment of teachers as it would mean additional burden on exchequer.

It is necessary, as perceived by the experts in education, for an institution to exist in ideal conditions. This requires not just sufficient infrastructure within the institution but also several other important facilities to be made available to the institution.

PART II

FINANCIAL GRIEVANCES

FIVE

Financial Grievances of the Minority Managed Educational Institutions

This chapter deals with the financial grievances related to the following areas which are related to funds and grants:

(a) Statewise financial grievances
(b) Religionwise financial grievances
(c) Type of institutionwise financial grievances

The following aspects related to the financial grievances have been studied here:

1. Source of Funds
2. Adequacy of Funds
3. Timely Release of Grants
4. Where Grants are held up
5. Efforts to get Grants
6. Areas Affected due to Delay in Grants
7. Utilization of Grants

Statewise Financial Grievances

Source of Funds

The statewise analysis of financial grievances of minority managed educational institutions in India had revealed that one-fourth to one-third of all minority institutions in Bihar, Maharashtra and Andhra Pradesh; and half, or, more than half of all minority institutions in Chandigarh, Gujarat, Kerala and Uttar Pradesh derive their source of funds only from the government (Table 5.1). Further, three-fourths of institutions in Mizoram and all institutions in Orissa have only government as their source of fund. All other states studied had insignificant proportions of institutions which have only government as their source of fund.

Another 33 per cent of institutions in Andhra Pradesh, and above, one-tenth of institutions in Karnataka and Maharashtra had only management as their source of funds. One-third of institutions in Andhra Pradesh indicate public contributions and donations as their source of funds.

Among the institutions which had both government and management as their source of funds, more than one-third of institutions in Tamil Nadu, one-fourth of institutions in Bihar, half of institutions in Delhi, one-fifth of institutions in Punjab, and all the institutions of Haryana are notable ones.

TABLE - 5.1
SOURCE OF FUNDS

(Percentage Distribution)

State/U.T.	*Govt.* (%)	*Management* (%)	*Public* (%)	*Govt. & Management* (%)	*Multiple Source* (%)	*Row Total* (%)	*%*	*Total for Each Row*
Andhra Pradesh	33	1	33	33	0	0	50	100
Bihar	25	0	0	0	25	50	15	100
Chandigarh	50	0	0	0	0	50	30	100
Delhi	0	0	0	0	50	50	57	100
Gujarat	67	0	0	0	0	33	18	100
Haryana	0	0	0	0	100	0	3	100
Karnataka	18	3	18	0	6	59	57	100
Kerala	67	0	0	0	0	33	61	100
Maharashtra	29	2	14	14	7	36	63	100
Mizoram	75	0	0	0	0	25	12	100
Orissa	100	0	0	0	0	0	9	100
Punjab	11	0	0	0	22	67	27	100
Tamil Nadu	9	0	0	0	36	56	66	100
Uttar Pradesh	67	0	0	0	0	33	36	100
West Bengal	0	0	0	0	0	0	3	100

Row total indicates the no. of questionnaires for each state (in all tables)

The states in which institutions had multiple sources of funds can be grouped into three categories. They are: (i) one-third of institutions of Gujarat, Kerala, Maharashtra and U.P. (ii) half of institutions in Bihar, Chandigarh, Delhi and Tamil Nadu and (iii) more than six-tenths of institutions in Karnataka and Punjab.

Adequacy of Funds

As far as the adequacy of funds is concerned, the management of one-fourth of institutions in U.P. and Karnataka, one-third and slightly above one-third of institutions in Orissa and Tamil Nadu have revealed that they are adequate to a great extent (Table 5.2). Half of the institutions in Chandigarh, Delhi and Gujarat, and more than six-tenths of institutions in Punjab had thought that the grants were adequate to a great extent.

Another one-fourth of institutions in Kerala, one-third of institutions in Maharashtra, Orissa and Punjab, and half of the institutions in Delhi, Gujarat, Mizoram and U.P. had felt that the grants were adequate to some extent only. All the institutions in Andhra Pradesh and West Bengal had also revealed that the grants were adequate to some extent only.

TABLE - 5.2
ADEQUACY OF FUNDS

(Percentage distribution)

State/U.T.	*Great Extent (%)*	*Some Extent (%)*	*Not at All (%)*	*(%) Row Total*	*% Total For Each Row*
Andhra Pradesh	0	100	0	30	100
Bihar	0	0	100	12	100
Chandigarh	50	0	50	30	100
Delhi	50	50	0	57	100
Gujarat	50	50	0	18	100
Haryana	0	0	0	3	100
Karnataka	23	46	31	57	100
Kerala	13	25	63	51	100
Maharashtra	10	30	60	63	100
Mizoram	0	50	50	12	100
Orissa	33	33	33	9	100
Punjab	67	33	0	27	100
Tamil Nadu	40	0	60	66	100
Uttar Pradesh	25	50	25	42	100
West Bengal	0	100	0	6	100

All the institutions studied in Bihar and more than six-tenths of the institutions in Kerala, Maharashtra and Tamil Nadu had categorically said that they were not at all adequate, whereas half of the institutions in Chandigarh and Mizoram, one-third of institutions in Orissa and Karnataka had expressed so.

Timely Release of Grants

All the institutions in Chandigarh and Haryana, and majority of the institutions in Tamil Nadu, Punjab, Orissa and Gujarat have stated that the grants reach them in time. About half of the institutions in Andhra Pradesh and Uttar Pradesh have also stated so (Table 5.3).

On the other hand, all the institutions in Bihar, Delhi and Mizoram had said that the grants did not reach them in time. The majority of the institutions in Karnataka, Kerala and Maharashtra also stated that the grants did not reach in time.

From all these three tables (5.1 to 5.3), it becomes evident that the grievances are dissimilar, or peculiar among the states and within the states. Financial grievances of minority institutions presumably assume locational features in the sense, that the source, adequacy and timely release of funds, by and large, depend on the locational advantage of the institution within the state.

TABLE - 5.3
TIMELY RELEASE OF GRANTS

(Percentage distribution)

Sl. No.	*State/U.T.*	*Yes (%)*	*No (%)*	*Row Total*	*% Total for Each Row*
1.	Andhra Pradesh	50	50	30	100
2.	Bihar	0	100	12	100
3.	Chandigarh	100	0	30	100
4.	Delhi	0	100	57	100
5.	Gujarat	67	33	18	100
6.	Haryana	100	0	3	100
7.	Karnataka	18	82	87	100
8.	Kerala	25	75	51	100
9.	Maharashtra	25	75	66	100
10.	Mizoram	0	100	12	100
11.	Orissa	67	33	9	100
12.	Punjab	75	25	27	100
13.	Tamil Nadu	88	13	66	100
14.	Uttar Pradesh	50	50	42	100
15.	West Bengal	0	0	6	100

Where Grants are held up

It was at 'State level', that the grants were generally held up was the reply of all the institutions in Gujarat, and majority of the institutions in Kerala, Maharashtra, Punjab, Tamil Nadu and Bihar, whereas only half of the institutions of U.P., and slightly above four-tenths of institutions in Karnataka would agree with this (Table 5.4).

TABLE - 5.4
PLACE WHERE GRANTS ARE HELD UP

(Percentage distribution)

Sl. No.	*State/U.T.*	*At State Level (%)*	*At District Level (%)*	*%*	*Any Other Level (%)*	*Row Total*	*% Total for Each Row*
1.	Andhra Pradesh	0	1	100	0	30	100
2.	Bihar	57	3	43	0	51	100
3.	Chandigarh	0	0	0	0	30	100
4.	Delhi	0	2	100	0	57	100
5.	Gujarat	100	0	0	0	18	100
6.	Haryana	0	0	0	0	3	100
7.	Karnataka	44	5	31	25	75	100
8.	Kerala	86	1	14	0	54	100
9.	Maharashtra	67	1	11	22	69	100
10.	Mizoram	33	1	33	33	15	100
11.	Orissa	0	0	0	0	9	100
12.	Punjab	60	1	20	20	30	100
13.	Tamil Nadu	60	2	40	0	66	100
14.	Uttar Pradesh	50	0	0	50	42	100
15.	West Bengal	0	0	0	0	6	100

All institutions in Andhra Pradesh and Delhi had said that they were delayed at the district level. One-third of institutions in Karnataka and Orissa, four-tenths of institutions in Punjab had also said that the grants were delayed at the district level.

Special Efforts to get Grants

In case of Andhra Pradesh, Bihar, Delhi, Kerala and Mizoram, all the institutions had to make special efforts to get grants. In addition, majority of the institutions in Karnataka, Tamil Nadu, Orissa and Maharashtra also expressed that they had to make special efforts to get grants in time. This was the reply for half of the institutions in Chandigarh and U.P. (Table 5.5).

On the other hand, in case of Gujarat and Haryana, no institution did make any special effort to get grants released in time. This was the reply for majority of the institutions in Punjab and half of the institutions in Chandigarh and U.P.

TABLE - 5.5
DISTRIBUTION OF SPECIAL EFFORTS TO GET GRANTS

(Percentage distribution)

Sl. No.	*State/U.T.*	*Yes (%)*	*No (%)*	*Row Total*	*% Total for Each Row*
1.	Andhra Pradesh	100	0	50	100
2.	Bihar	100	0	12	100
3.	Chandigarh	50	50	30	100
4.	Delhi	100	0	57	100
5.	Gujarat	0	100	18	100
6.	Haryana	0	100	3	100
7.	Karnataka	92	8	57	100
8.	Kerala	100	0	51	100
9.	Maharashtra	58	42	66	100
10.	Mizoram	100	0	12	100
11.	Orissa	67	33	9	100
12.	Punjab	38	63	27	100
13.	Tamil Nadu	63	38	66	100
14.	Uttar Pradesh	50	50	39	100
15.	West Bengal	0	0	9	100

Delay in Receipt of Grants

In Delhi, the fund was always delayed for all institutions, and in states like Andhra Pradesh and Bihar it was either "always" or "very often" the fund was delayed (Table 5.6).

For majority of the institutions in Karnataka and Kerala the fund was delayed either 'always' or 'very often'. Half of the institutions in Tamil Nadu and one-third of institutions in Gujarat also had said, that the funds were delayed 'always'. For majority of the institutions in Mizoram the fund was delayed 'very often'.

The grants from the government are only delayed 'some time' for any institution in Chandigarh, Haryana and Orissa. The majority of the institutions in Gujarat, Maharashtra, Punjab and Uttar Pradesh reported that they experienced the delay in receipt of funds only 'some time'.

Areas Affected due to Delay in Receipt of Grants

In Andhra Pradesh, the areas, such as salaries of the staff, maintenance of the building, scholarships, teaching aids, and sports activities got effected in almost equal proportion, in all institutions, due to delay in receipt of grants. In Bihar, it is maintenance of the building, teaching aids and sports activities; in Chandigarh, only salaries of the staff; in Delhi, it is maintenance of the building (half of the institutions), scholarships and teaching aids; in Gujarat, it is teaching aids, scholarships, salaries of the staff and sports activities; in Haryana, only salaries of the staff; in Karnataka, it is salaries of the staff, maintenance of the building, scholarship, teaching aids. In Kerala, it is maintenance of the building for more than six-tenths of institutions in addition to scholarships and teaching aids, in Maharashtra; it is maintenance of the building, and teaching aids; in Mizoram, it is salaries of the staff, maintenance of the building, scholarships and sports activities which got affected (Table 5.7).

TABLE - 5.6
DELAY IN RECEIPT OF GRANTS

(Percentage distribution)

Sl. No.	*State/U.T.*	*Always (%)*	*Very Often (%)*	*Some Time (%)*	*On Rare Occasions (%)*	*%*	*Row Total*	*% Total for each Row*
1.	Andhra Pradesh	50	50	0	0	0	30	100
2.	Bihar	75	25	0	0	0	12	100
3.	Chandigarh	0	0	100	0	0	30	100
4.	Delhi	100	0	0	0	0	57	100
5.	Gujarat	33	0	67	0	0	18	100
6.	Haryana	0	0	100	0	0	3	100
7.	Karnataka	42	25	33	0	0	57	100
8.	Kerala	50	25	25	0	0	48	100
9.	Maharashtra	27	0	64	1	0	69	100
10.	Mizoram	0	75	25	0	0	12	100
11.	Orissa	0	0	100	0	0	9	100
12.	Punjab	25	0	75	0	0	27	100
13.	Tamil Nadu	50	0	50	0	0	66	100
14.	Uttar Pradesh	0	33	67	0	0	42	100
15.	West Bengal	0	0	0	0	0	6	100

To sum up, salaries of the staff were being affected in large proportion of institutions, in many states, to be followed by scholarships, and maintenance of the building. A considerable proportion of the institutions reported that teaching aids and sports activities also got affected.

TABLE - 5.7
AREAS AFFECTED DUE TO DELAY IN RECEIPT OF GRANTS

(Percentage distribution)

Sl. No.	*State/U.T.*	*Salaries of the Staff (%)*	*Mainte-nance & Bldg. (%)*	*Scho-lar-ships (%)*	*Teach-ing Aids (%)*	*Sports Activi-ties (%)*	*Any Other (%)*	*Row Total*	*Total for Each Row (%)*
1.	Andhra Pradesh	29	14	14	14	14	14	45	100
2.	Bihar	10	30	0	30	30	0	30	100
3.	Chandigarh	100	0	0	0	0	0	30	100
4.	Delhi	50	0	25	25	0	0	63	100
5.	Gujarat	18	0	24	29	18	12	54	100
6.	Haryana	100	0	0	0	0	0	3	100
7.	Karnataka	29	16	23	16	13	3	111	100
8.	Kerala	0	64	21	14	0	0	66	100
9.	Maharashtra	10	22	12	22	17	17	159	100
10.	Mizoram	30	20	20	10	20	0	30	100
11.	Orissa	9	27	27	18	18	0	33	100
12.	Punjab	19	5	24	24	24	5	66	100
13.	Tamil Nadu	20	30	10	20	10	10	78	100
14.	Uttar Pradesh	27	18	18	18	9	9	63	100
15.	West Bengal	0	0	0	0	0	0	6	100

Utilization of Funds

When the heads of institutions in the different States were asked whether funds received by the institution were utilized properly, uniformly all the institutions in Andhra Pradesh, Bihar, Chandigarh, Delhi, Gujarat, Haryana, Karnataka, Mizoram, Tamil Nadu and Uttar Pradesh had said that they were utilized properly. The majority of the institutions in Kerala, Maharashtra, Orissa and Punjab had also agreed that the funds were utilized properly (Table 5.8).

Suggestions of Teaching Staff to Improve Minority Managed Educational Institutions

When various suggestions to improve the conditions of minority managed educational institutions were mentioned for the teaching staff to give their opinion, almost similar proportion of teaching staff of Christian, Buddhist and Parsi institutions attached equal importance to suggestions like 'Adequate allocation'

'Timely Release' and 'effective utilization' of grants, unbiased selection and punctuality on the part of teaching and non-teaching staff, better teaching facilities and improved working conditions (Table 5.9).

TABLE - 5.8
OPINION ON UTILIZATION OF FUNDS

(Percentage distribution)

Sl. No.	*State/U.T.*	*Yes (%)*	*No (%)*	*Row Total*	*% Total for Each Row*
1.	Andhra Pradesh	100	0	30	100
2.	Bihar	100	0	12	100
3.	Chandigarh	100	0	30	100
4.	Delhi	100	0	57	100
5.	Gujarat	100	0	18	100
6.	Haryana	100	0	3	100
7.	Karnataka	100	0	57	100
8.	Kerala	89	11	51	100
9.	Maharashtra	83	17	75	100
10.	Mizoram	100	0	12	100
11.	Orissa	75	25	12	100
12.	Punjab	70	30	33	100
13.	Tamil Nadu	100	0	66	100
14.	Uttar Pradesh	100	0	39	100
15.	West Bengal	0	100	6	100

The teaching staff of the Sikh institutions considered only adequate allocation, unbiased selection of teaching staff and improved working conditions were important. Half of the teaching staff considered adequate allocation of grants as necessary to improve the condition.

The majority of the teaching staff of the Muslim institutions have not considered punctuality of teaching and non-teaching staff, better teaching facilities, improved working condition and unbiased selection as necessary. They mentioned that only 'adequate allocation' and 'timely release of grants' were necessary steps towards the improvement of minority education. It becomes clear from the table, as it is understood by the teaching staff of any minority managed educational institution that adequate allocation and timely release of grants stand out as significant suggestions to improve the situation.

TABLE - 5.9

SUGGESTIONS OF TEACHING STAFF TO IMPROVE M.M.E. INSTITUTIONS

(Percentage distribution)

Sl. No.	Religious Minority	Adequate Allocation (%)	Timely Release (%)	Effective Utilization (%)	Teaching Staff (%)	Non-Teaching Staff (%)	Better Teaching Facilities (%)	Improved Working Condition (%)	Unbiased Selection of Teaching Staff (%)	Row Total	Total for Each Row (%)
1.	Muslim	31	42	9	1	0	0	4	12	480	100
2.	Christian	17	14	11	11	15	13	18	1	375	100
3.	Sikh	55	0	0	0	0	0	15	30	87	100
4.	Buddhist	13	11	11	7	16	13	18	11	141	100
5.	Parsi	10	10	10	13	13	13	13	17	99	100

TABLE - 5.10

SOURCE OF FUNDS

(Percentage distribution)

Sl. No.	Religious Minority	Government (%)	Management (%)	Public (%)	Government & Management (%)	Multiple Sources (%)	Row Total	Total for each Row (%)
1.	Muslim	30	6	8	15	42	291	100
2.	Christian	33	13	0	13	46	75	100
3.	Sikh	13	0	0	25	63	81	100
4.	Buddhist	33	0	0	0	67	42	100
5.	Parsi	50	17	0	0	33	24	100

There was a misconception that the adequate grants would take care of most of the prevailing ills and weaknesses of these institutions; and these institutions will be able to serve meaningful purpose. Strangely enough, this kind of misconception prevails largely among the Muslim minority managed educational institutions. Largely, the responses coming from various groups of these institutions expect financial support from the project funds. They have some deep seated thinking in the mind that in terms of allocation of funds they are at a disadvantage. Therefore, they try to discover all weaknesses and ills of the institution in the inadequacy of finances, and tend to overlook other important areas which need utmost attention, such as, punctuality of the teaching and non-teaching staff, unbiased selection, and the like. It cannot be denied that finances are basic to improve the working conditions, but punctuality, improved teaching, quality of education could not follow from finances alone. It is optimistic to note that the minority institutions other than the Muslim see the value of finances as well as other aspects of education in a balanced manner; while most of the Muslim minority managed educational institutions tend to see that if adequate grants are available, all other weaknesses will be taken care of by the management. So, the point they stress so much is of liberal financial grants to the minority managed educational institutions from the government. They view that providing grants is the responsibility of the government, while at the same time, administering an institution is purely an affair of the management which should be at liberty to do anything at its sweet will. These institutions are not willing to accept even reasonable regulations to maintain the standard of education, and to provide purely quality education to minorities.

Religionwise Financial Grievances

Source of Funds

According to Table 5.10, source of funds, among the Muslim managed educational institutions; three-tenths reported government as their only source of funds, while more than fourth-tenths reported to have multiple sources of funds. More or less similar trend is exhibited among the Christian institutions. The majority of Buddhist institutions studied reported to have multiple sources, while most of the Parsi institutions have either government or management as their only source of funds.

Among all minority managed educational institutions, Muslim institutions constitute more than half in various sources of funds, obviously due to differential samples taken in each religious category. It is to be particularly noted that all the institutions which reported 'public' as their only source of funds are only Muslim institutions.

Government, public donations, to some extent management, and in some cases donations from outside agencies are the sources of funds to the minority managed educational institutions.

Adequacy of Funds

Only about one-fifth of all Muslim institutions, around one-third of all Christian institutions, and one-fourth of Parsi institutions reported that the grants they received were adequate to a great extent. Three-fifths of all Sikh institutions had reported that they were adequate, to a great extent. A majority of the Christian institutions and half of the Parsi institutions felt that the grants were not at all adequate, while more than two-fifths of Muslim and Buddhist institutions have said that the grants were not at all adequate (Table 5.11).

TABLE - 5.11
ADEQUACY OF FUNDS

(Percentage distribution)

Sl. No.	*Religious Minority*	*Great Extent (%)*	*Some Extent (%)*	*Not at All (%)*	*Row Total*	*Total for Each Row (%)*
1.	Muslim	20	39	41	288	100
2.	Christian	60	10	60	69	100
3.	Sikh	60	30	10	75	100
4.	Buddhist	0	57	43	30	100
5.	Parsi	25	25	50	24	100

Almost all minority managed educational institutions complained of the inadequacy of grants; only about one-fourth to one-fifth of them view that the grants received by them are somewhat adequate. The allocation of grants is the crucial area where the grievances accumulate and mount irrespective of the religious group, state or region and type of institutions. The minority managed institutions almost uniformally maintained that inadequacy of funding is the basic source of their main grievance.

Timely Release of Grants

Side by side with the inadequacy of funding, delay in the release of funds is another cause of grievance among these institutions (Table 5.12).

TABLE - 5.12
TIMELY RELEASE OF GRANTS

(Percentage distribution)

Sl. No.	*Religious Minority*	*Yes (%)*	*No (%)*	*Row Total*	*% Total for Each Row*
1.	Muslim	40	60	288	100
2.	Christian	36	64	69	100
3.	Sikh	60	40	75	100
4.	Buddhist	0	100	30	100
5.	Parsi	50	50	24	100

Generally, majority of all minority managed educational institutions reported that the grants from the government do not reach in time. In case of Buddhist institutions, it is to be particularly noted that all of them had reported that the grants do not reach them timely, whereas the experience of about three-fifths of all Sikh institutions, and about half of the Parsi institutions is different as they reported that the grants received from the government reach in time. During our deeper investigations it transpired that of all types of grants given by the government, the release of maintenance grants is always delayed by the various State Governments, although it is not peculiar to only minority managed educational institutions. Other non-minority institutions in the area also suffer a similar experience.

As far as the release of maintenance grants is concerned, the minority institutions vis-a-vis the non-minority institutions are on a par. They suffer equally on account of delay in our system.

Where Grants are Held Up

It has been reported that grants are held up generally at the State level. About every 7 out of 10 Muslim and Sikh institutions, half of the Buddhist institutions, about four-fifths of Christian institutions, and all Parsi institutions had reported that the grants are held up at state level. This situation arises because of the general condition prevailing in State Governments that the grants to educational institutions get often delayed due to paucity of funds (Table 5.13).

TABLE - 5.13
PLACE WHERE GRANTS ARE HELD UP

(Percentage distribution)

Sl. No.	Religious Minority	At State Level (%)	At District Level (%)	Any other Level (%)	Row Total	% Total for Each Row
1.	Muslim	73	12	15	288	100
2.	Christian	89	0	11	69	100
3.	Sikh	71	14	14	75	100
4.	Buddhist	50	25	25	30	100
5.	Parsi	100	0	0	25	100

Special Efforts to Get Grants

Majority of the minority managed educational institutions reported that they often make special efforts to get grants in time with an exception of Sikh institutions of which only half of them reported to do so. Only about one-fifth of Christian, one-fourth of Parsi and about two-fifths of Muslim institutions reported as not making any special efforts to get grants released in time. While 50 per cent of the Sikh institutions reported as not making any special efforts; on the contrary, all the Buddhist institutions had reported as making special efforts to get grants in time (Table 5.14).

TABLE - 5.14
WHETHER ANY SPECIAL EFFORTS ARE MADE TO GET GRANTS

(Percentage distribution)

Sl. No.	Religious Minority	Yes (%)	No (%)	Row Total	% Total for Each Row
1.	Muslim	63	37	288	100
2.	Christian	90	10	69	100
3.	Sikh	50	50	75	100
4.	Buddhist	100	0	30	100
5.	Parsi	75	25	24	100

By and large, the various minority institutions have to make extra efforts to get the grants released. This practice breeds corruption and delay. It must be ensured that grants are released within a definite period without having the institutions to approach for the release of grants.

Delay in receipt of grants

With regard to how often funds are delayed for minority managed educational institutions, a little more than three-fifths of Muslim and Christian institutions have either reported 'always' or 'very often' (Table 5.15). The majority of the Buddhist institutions have just reported 'very often' fund is delayed. On the contrary about one-fourth of the Parsi institutions and a little less than one-fourth of the Sikh institutions had said that the fund is delayed either 'Always' or 'very often', while a great majority of these institutions had reported that the delay is either 'some time' or on 'rare occasions'.

Delay is part of the process. This is the most crucial cause of accumulation of grievance. All policy and administrative initiative must see how to avoid delay.

TABLE - 5.15
DELAY IN RECEIPT OF GRANTS

(Percentage distribution)

Sl. No.	*Religious Minority*	*Always (%)*	*Very Often (%)*	*Some Time (%)*	*On Rare Occasions (%)*	*Row Total*	*% Total for Each Row*
1.	Muslim	34	18	42	5	288	100
2.	Christian	55	9	27	9	69	100
3.	Sikh	23	0	62	15	75	100
4.	Buddhist	0	60	40	0	30	100
5.	Parsi	25	0	75	0	24	100

Areas affected due to delay in release of grants

By and large, educational institutions receive three types of grants from the State Governments. They are salary grants for teaching and non-teaching staff which is directly paid to the employees in many states, and in which case the delay is nil or minimal; the maintenance grants for expenditures on maintenance of building, teaching aids, sports activities and for any other recurring expenditures; and lastly scholarship grants in various schemes in different states to benefit the students. The higher and professional education institutions, such as, arts and science colleges and professional colleges also receive various grants from their parent bodies. This study attempted to see the areas which got affected due to delay in disbursement of grants which are given broadly to benefit employees, institutions and students (Table 5.16).

TABLE - 5.16
AREAS AFFECTED DUE TO DELAY IN RECEIPT OF GRANTS

(Percentage distribution)

Sl. No.	*Religious Minority*	*Salaries* (%)	*Maintenance* (%)	*Scholarships* (%)	*Teaching Aids* (%)	*Sports Activities* (%)	*Any Other* (%)	*Row Total*	*Total for Each Row*
1.	Muslim	27	32	32	3	3	3	174	100
2.	Christian	9	73	9	0	0	9	66	100
3.	Sikh	57	0	43	0	0	0	51	100
4.	Buddhist	26	21	11	16	21	5	69	100
5.	Parsi	0	25	25	19	19	13	60	100

Table 5.16 shows that the major areas affected due to delay in disbursement of grants are salaries of the staff, maintenance of the building, and scholarships although the ratio of institutions which got affected is little less than one-fourth in salaries of the staff, and about one-third in maintenance of the building and scholarships. On the contrary, in about three-fourths of the Christian institutions, maintenance of the building gets affected. The larger proportion of even Buddhist and Parsi institutions reported that maintenance of building got affected followed by more or less similar proportion of these institutions which suffered in the area of scholarships due to delay in disbursement of grants. The Sikh institutions with some exception reported that only salaries of the staff and scholarship got affected.

It is to be taken into account here that generally the release of maintenance grants got affected for most of the institutions but the areas affected at the institution in many cases have no direct rela-tionship with the delay in a particular type of grant, and institutions which often went into the practice of using the fund of one head which is actually meant for the other. Hence, in order for an institution to enable optimum use of funds for the purpose it is given, it is to be taken care that all types of grants get released in time.

The delay in release of grants has its repercussions and change effects on various other areas of activity. Thus, the grievances arise and accumulate.

Utilization of Grants

The heads of institutions of minority managed educational institutions, invariably major proportions of them, affirm that the funds to their institutions are utilized properly, while, just one-fourth of Parsi institutions have mentioned that the funds are not utilized properly (Table 5.17).

TABLE - 5.17
OPINION ON UTILIZATION OF FUNDS

(Percentage distribution)

Sl. No.	*Religious Minority*	*Yes (%)*	*No (%)*	*Row Total*	*% Total for Each Row*
1.	Muslim	93	7	288	100
2.	Christian	100	0	69	100
3.	Sikh	92	8	75	100
4.	Buddhist	86	14	30	100
5.	Parsi	75	25	24	100

It was difficult for us to judge whether the funds were utilized properly as claimed by majority of the institutions. However, effective and proper utilization of funds is crucial to the improvement in the educational scenario of the minority managed educational institutions.

Areas Affected due to Delay in Grants

Not proper utilization of grants by the institution is often quoted as one of the reasons in the government authorities circles for any delay in release of grants. In some regions, government authorities maintain that the practice of not proper utilization of grants was adopted by the management of institution concerned (Table 5.18). When the heads of the institutions were asked to reply on areas affected due to improper utilization of grants which is an offshoot of the earlier question, and thereby assumes less significance as insignificant number of institutions reported different affected areas. However small the number be, one-third of Parsi institutions and one-fifth of Sikh institutions had reported that salaries of the staff got affected due to improper utilization. More than one-tenth of Sikh, Buddhist, Parsi institutions also reported that maintenance of the building got affected due to improper utilization of grants. As it was said earlier, it became clear, that many institutions used their funds for different purposes interchangeably because of scarcity of resources.

TABLE - 5.18

AREAS AFFECTED DUE TO IMPROPER UTILIZATION OF GRANTS

(Percentage distribution)

Sl. No.	*Religious Minority*	*Salaries of the Staff (%)*	*Maintenance of the Building (%)*	*Scholarships (%)*	*Teaching Aids (%)*	*Sports Activities (%)*	*Any Other (%)*	*Row Total*	*% Total for Each Row*
1.	Muslim	3	7	6	6	1	2	303	100
2.	Christian	0	9	0	0	0	0	69	100
3.	Sikh	20	12	0	0	0	0	75	100
4.	Buddhist	0	17	8	8	0	0	36	100
5.	Parsi	33	11	0	0	0	0	27	100

The grants received on various heads were generally diverted and used for making payment of salaries. There were also instances where diversion of fund was made for use on other heads than salary. Even payment of salary was delayed. In the event of scarcity of fund, diversion of grants from one head to another, sometimes for the sake of real need of the institution, and sometimes at the discretion of the managing committee, or head of the institution was a usual phenomenon.

Opinion of the Teaching Staff in Minority Managed Educational Institutions

It is often said that meritorious persons do not find place in minority managed educational institutions because of their exclusivity. When the teaching staff of these institutions were asked to give their comment on whether the meritorious did not get opportunity in (i) management (ii) teaching staff; and (iii) non-teaching staff; more or less six-tenths of Christian, Sikh and Buddhist institutions had agreed that the meritorious did not find place in management, while only less than half of the teaching staff of the Muslim institutions think so (Table 5.19).

TABLE - 5.19
OPINION (TEACHING STAFF) ON OPPORTUNITIES IN M.M.E. INSTITUTIONS

(Percentage distribution)

Sl. No.	*Religious Minority*	*Management Position (%)*	*Teaching Position (%)*	*Non-Teaching Position (%)*	*Total for Each Row*	*% Total for Each Row*
1.	Muslim	42	34	24	354	100
2.	Christian	67	33	0	69	100
3.	Sikh	60	20	20	75	100
4.	Buddhist	57	29	14	36	100
5.	Parsi	14	57	29	33	100

As far as the opportunity for the meritorious people to the teaching position is concerned, more or less one-third of Muslim, Christian and Buddhist institutions, and more than half of the teaching staff of the Parsi institutions had reported that the meritorious did not get opportunity. More or less a similar trend, though at a less proportion was exhibited for non-teaching staff position.

This is so because, the working conditions of teaching and and non-teaching staff in these institutions is not attractive. Often there is underpayment or late payment of salaries and allowances. The influential members of the management often favour their own kith and kin, near and dear ones or their own men. This is generally so in case of non-teaching staff. In this respect, minority managed educational institutions, and other institutions, purely privately managed, suffer from similar weaknesses and handicaps.

Type of Institutionwise Financial Grievances

- Pri-School - includes primary, upper primary or middle school
- H.S. School - includes high school, secondary school and higher secondary school, pre-university or inter college.
- Degree College - includes all Arts, Science and Commerce colleges.
- P.G. College - includes all Postgraduate colleges
- Prof./Tech. - includes all Professional colleges like Medical, Teacher Training, Engineering and Technical Institutes like ITI, Polytechnics.

Source of funds

The majority of primary and upper primary schools have multiple sources of funds with less than one-fifth of all such schools depending on the government for resources; on the other hand, more or less one-third of higher secondary school, degree and postgraduate colleges depending upon only government for funds. Another 36 per cent of higher secondary schools and four-tenths of degree and postgraduate colleges have multiple sources of funds. Equal proportions of six-tenths of professional and technical institutions depend either on government or management or multiple sources, while another four-tenths derive their sources from public (Table 5.20).

TABLE - 5.20

SOURCES OF FUNDS TYPE OF INSTITUTIONWISE GRIEVANCE

(Percentage distribution)

Sl. No.	*Type of the Institution*	*Govt.*	*Management*	*Public*	*Govt. & Management*	*Multiple Sources*	*Row Total*	*% Total for each Row*
1.	Pri School	17	8	13	0	63	105	100
2.	H.S. School	38	8	6	12	36	243	100
3.	Dgr. College	33	0	25	0	42	69	100
4.	P.G. College	30	0	0	30	40	45	100
5.	Prof/Tech	20	20	40	0	20	27	100

Adequacy of funds

For 90% of the primary and upper primary minority managed schools the funds are either adequate to 'some extent' or they are 'not at all adequate'. As far as the higher secondary school, degree and postgraduate colleges are concerned, the proportions of the institutions reported in "Great Extent" increase from higher secondary school to postgraduate college with lower limit of one-fourth of higher secondary school, and upper limit of four-tenths of postgraduate college. The trend is more or less the same at "some extent", whereas it reversed at "Not at all" category, with one-fifth of postgraduate institutions and more than four-tenths of higher secondary schools. All professional institutions studied had reported that the funds are not at all adequate (Table 5.21).

TABLE - 5.21
ADEQUACY OF FUNDS

(Percentage distribution)

Sl. No.	*Type of the Institution*	*Great. Extent*	*Some Extent*	*Not at All*	*Row Total*	*Total for Each Row (%)*
1.	Pri School	9	45	45	105	100
2.	H.S. School	25	30	45	243	100
3.	Dgr. College	36	27	36	64	100
4.	P.G. College	44	33	22	45	100
5.	Prof/Tech	0	0	100	27	100

Timely release of grants

The grant from the government does not reach in time for all the professional institutions, and about nine-tenths of primary and upper primary schools of the minorities. It reaches in time only for more than four-tenths of secondary and higher secondary schools, six-tenths of Degree colleges and seven-tenths of post-graduate colleges (Table 5.22).

TABLE - 5.22
TIMELY RELEASE OF GRANTS

(Percentage distribution)

Sl. No.	*Type of the Institution*	*Yes*	*No*	*Row Total*	*% Total for Each Row*
1.	Pri School	9	91	105	100
2.	H.S. School	44	56	243	100
3.	Dgr. College	60	40	69	100
4.	P.G. College	70	30	45	100
5.	Prof./Tech.	0	100	27	100

Where Grants are Held Up

It is at the state level for all the professional institutions; and for more or less three-fourths of the upper primary schools and higher secondary schools and half of the degree colleges, the fund is held up at the state level (Table 5.23).

For the rest of the primary schools and higher secondary schools and one-third of the degree colleges, the fund is held up at the district level.

The Table 5.23 more or less confirms our earlier findings that insufficient allocation of funds at the disposal of State Governments results in inadequacy of funds, and delay in releasing funds, which occur for most of the institutions at the State level. However, the perception of the management on the procedural delay at various places varies.

TABLE - 5.23
WHERE GRANTS ARE HELD UP

(Percentage distribution)

Sl. No.	*Type of the Institution*	*State Level*	*At District Level*	*%*	*Row Total*	*% Total for Each Row*
1.	Pri. School	71	29	0	105	100
2.	H.S. School	78	22	0	243	100
3.	Dgr. College	50	33	17	69	100
4.	P.G. College	57	14	29	45	100
5.	Prof/Tech	100	0	0	27	100

Special Efforts to Get Grants

On deeper probe into the delay in disbursement of grants to the institutions, six-tenths of postgraduate colleges, seven-tenths of professional, secondary and higher secondary schools, and eight-tenths of primary and upper primary schools reported that they made special efforts in order to get grants released in time (Table 5.24). The exception being some degree colleges in which more than six-tenths of them reported that they did not make any special effort to get grants released in time. Generally urban or township situation of the degree colleges may be advantageous to them. For them, delay is minimal because of their proximity to the administrative offices at the regional, district and state level.

TABLE - 5.24
SPECIAL EFFORTS TO GET GRANTS

(Percentage distribution)

Sl. No.	*Type of the Institution*	*Yes*	*No*	*Row Total*	*% Total for Each Row*
1.	Pri School	82	18	105	100
2.	H.S. School	74	26	243	100
3.	Dgr. College	33	67	69	100
4.	P.G. College	60	40	45	100
5.	Prof/Tech	67	33	27	100

How often Funds are Delayed

The delay in receipt of grants by the institution can be 'always' or 'very often' due to delay in bureaucratic functioning, or also due to non-availability of funds at the state or district level. It can be only 'some times' or on 'rare occasions' due to unavoidable reasons (Table 5.25).

TABLE - 5.25
HOW OFTEN FUND IS DELAYED

(Percentage distribution)

Sl. No.	*Type of the Institution*	*Always (%)*	*Very Often (%)*	*Some Time (%)*	*On Rare Occasions (%)*	*Row Total*	*Total for Each Row (%)*
1.	Pri. School	44	11	44	0	105	100
2.	H.S. School	38	18	43	3	243	100
3.	Dgr. College	10	30	60	0	69	100
4.	P.G. College	33	0	67	0	45	100
5.	Prof/Tech	100	0	0	0	27	100

The study, in an effort to find out how often fund is delayed, observed that all professional and technical institutions, four-tenths of primary and upper primary schools, more than one-third of higher secondary schools, and one-third of postgraduate colleges 'always' experienced delay.

For about six-tenths of degree colleges and seven-tenths of postgraduate colleges delay is only sometime.

Areas Affected due to Delay in Receipt of Grants

When the grants for an institution are delayed, under normal circumstances, it would be the particular area for which the institution is to get grants which will be affected. However, the temporary arrangements of using different funds meant for different purposes are becoming the order of the day in educational institutions (Table 5.26).

TABLE - 5.26
AREAS AFFECTED DUE TO DELAY IN RECEIPT OF GRANTS

(Percentage distribution)

Sl. No.	*Type of the Institution*	*Salaries of the Staff*	*Main-tenance of the Building*	*Scholar-ships*	*Teaching Aids*	*Sports Activi-ties*	*Any Other*	*Row Total*	*Total for Each Row*
1.	Pri. School	24	24	18	21	12	3	297	100
2.	H.S. School	19	22	20	22	18	0	417	100
3.	Dgr. College	30	4	22	17	22	0	105	100
4.	P.G. College	23	38	8	23	8	0	57	100
5.	Prof/Tech	11	22	11	22	11	22	48	100

It becomes evident in the study that due to delay in receipt of funds, between one-fourth and one-fifth of primary, upper primary, secondary and higher secondary schools get affected in areas like 'salaries of the staff', 'maintenance of the building', 'scholarship', 'teaching aids', and 'sports activities'.

For less than one-fourth of degree colleges 'teaching aids', 'scholarship' and 'sport activities' get affected. In three-tenths of such institutions, salaries of the staff get delayed.

For most of postgraduate colleges the main areas affected are 'salaries of the staff', 'maintenance of the building' and 'teaching aids'.

Slightly more than one-fifth of professional and technical institutions get affected in 'maintenance of the building' and 'teaching aids'; while one-tenth of them get affected in salaries of the staff, scholarships and 'sports activities'.

Utilization of funds

The study, in an attempt to find out the effective utilization of funds by the managements of minority institutions, enquired from the heads of institutions whether funds received by the institution were utilized properly (Table 5.27).

TABLE - 5.27

OPINION (HEAD OF INST.) ON UTILIZATION OF FUNDS

(Percentage distribution)

Sl. No.	*Type of the Institution*	*Yes (%)*	*No (%)*	*Row Total*	*% Total for Each Row*
1.	Pri. School	71	29	105	100
2.	H.S. School	87	13	243	100
3.	Dgr. College	87	13	69	100
4.	P.G. College	100	0	45	100
5.	Prof/Tech	100	0	27	100

As per Table 5.27, in all the professional, technical institutions and postgraduate colleges, it was revealed that they were utilized properly. The majority of the primary, upper primary, secondary, higher secondary schools and degree colleges also reported that they were utilized properly.

Suggestions of Teaching Staff to Improve Minority Managed Educational Institutions

The teaching staff of various types of institutions had suggested uniform steps for the development of minority managed educational institutions (Table 5.28). Almost uniformly, equal proportions of teaching staff have attached equal importance to suggestions, like:

(i) adequate allocation of funds,
(ii) timely release of funds,
(iii) effective utilization of funds,
(iv) unbiased selection of teaching and non-teaching staff,
(v) punctuality of teaching and non-teaching staff,
(vi) better teaching facilities, and
(vii) improved working conditions.

Opportunity for Meritorious in Minority Managed Educational Institutions

The study observed that in four-tenths to five-tenths of all types of institutions, the meritorious do not get opportunity in their management positions (Table 5.29).

Another three-tenths to four-tenths of the teaching staff of all types of minority institutions reported that the meritorious do not get opportunity in 'teaching position'.

One-fourth to one-fifth of teaching staff of all types of institutions also revealed that at their institutions meritorious do not get opportunity in 'non-teaching position'.

Though the general trend may be as stated above, it is to be noted that about various teaching and non-teaching positions the observations made by the respondents may not be uniformly correct.

The colleges and other institutions most of them being managed by Christian societies; or Muslim societies tended to become beds of many types of abuses, one of which was that many teachers were not paid their salaries for months together. (Towards the end of 1971, private college teachers in the state of Kerala had gone on a ten-week strike to bring their grievances to the notice of the public.)

On February 18, 1972, the editorial of *The Times of India,*

TABLE - 5.28

SUGGESTION OF TEACHING STAFF TO IMPROVE M.M.E. INSTITUTIONS

(Percentage distribution)

Sl. No.	Type of the Institution	Adequate Allocation (%)	Timely Release (%)	Effective Utilisation (%)	Teaching Staff (%)	Non-teaching Staff (%)	Better Teaching Facilities (%)	Improved Working Condition (%)	Unbiased Selection of Teaching Staff (%)	Row Total	Total for Each Row (%)
1.	Pri. School	12	11	12	12	14	14	14	13	474	100
2.	H.S. School	14	13	10	10	13	13	15	13	1155	100
3.	Dgr. College	13	13	10	12	12	12	13	13	309	100
4.	P.G. College	15	15	10	11	14	15	14	6	219	100
5.	Prof/Tech	13	13	13	11	13	11	13	13	123	100

TABLE - 5.29

OPINION (TEACHING STAFF) ON OPPORTUNITIES IN M.M.E. INSTITUTIONS

(Percentage distribution)

Sl. No.	Type of the Institution	Management (%)	Teaching Position (%)	Non-Teaching Position (%)	Total Row	% Total for Each Row
1.	Pri. School	45	35	20	132	100
2.	H.S. School	36	39	25	294	100
3.	Dgr. College	38	31	31	87	100
4.	P.G. College	50	25	25	57	100
5.	Prof/Tech	40	40	20	30	100

commented that the way educational institutions were run by many of the Christian and Muslim societies of Kerala, under the protection of Article 30 of the Constitution, was an abuse of the Article, and if, the institutions were not set right by their Christian or Muslim managements, they could not escape some diminution in "their hitherto inviolable freedom" by merely raising the cry of "minority rights in danger".

Mr H.R. Gokhale (the then Minister) also remarked that certain Constitutional rights of the minorities were standing in the way of educational reform; and these minority rights in education might have to be curbed to end abuses.

In reaction, the General Secretary of the Muslim League declared that "the Muslim Community would not tolerate any attempt to abridge the rights of the minorities in violation of the assurance given by the Prime Minister during the debate on the 24th Amendment of the Constitution."

The basic point is, whether and how long the educational interest of the weaker sections among the minorities could be allowed to suffer at the hands of the more affluent and dominant groups among them, under the guise of certain Constitutional safeguards. In fact, these Constitutional safeguards, which were provided for the improvement and betterment of the social-educational conditions of these people, have turned out to be weapons to be used against them by the vested interests among these communities. These rots need to be stemmed; these abuses need to be corrected. More safeguards need to be provided against the existing safeguards which have gradually turned unsafe.

SIX

Financial Grievances Aggregated

An overview of the financial grievances of the minority managed educational institutions statewise is presented here. While some grievances are common and universal; some are specific to a particular state situation.

Andhra Pradesh

(i) Financial aid was not generally given to the minority educational institutions without much trouble, was the grievance of the Muslim minority educational institutions.

(ii) Discrimination against the Muslim minority educational institutions in allocation, sanctioning and releasing of grants was alleged. Some officials mentioned that there was no discrimination on the basis of religion. At the government level there was delay in some cases but the reasons could be (a) red tapism, (b) bureaucratic attitude or, (c) some other factor.

(iii) Grants were inadequate and always delayed.

(iv) Non-receipt of scholarship, book grants, study material were alleged by students.

(v) Government's insistence on Corpus fund for the recognition of the minority institution should be abdicated.

(vi) There is one case of Holy Fatima Oriental High School, Hyderabad, to which the grants-in-aid were released for four months only in 1989-90. Since March 1990, the teachers of this school were not getting any salary.

Bihar

(i) The salary of the teaching and non-teaching staff was delayed for months together. Arrears were not paid; and such situation prevailed in almost all institutions run by the minorities, and also other institutions.

(ii) No aid or maintenance grant was available to the Muslim Minority College (Bhagalpur) from either Government or University Grants Commission although the college is affiliated to the degree level.

(iii) Scholarships were not made available to students.

(iv) Grants-in-aid were delayed abnormally.

(v) Teachers in minority educational institutions did not get government's pay-scale, and disparity in service conditions existed.

(vi) Full salary was not paid in many of the minority institutions. If ten teachers were working in a school and six posts were approved, salary grants received for approved posts of teachers were adjusted in such a manner that the salary was paid to all teachers. Therefore, the full scale was not given to the teachers.

Chandigarh

(i) The teachers were not being paid properly and regularly. They received less than the prescribed pay.

(ii) Grants were not regular.

(iii) Students did not receive scholarships in time.

Delhi

(i) Lack of adequate and timely release of grants was alleged.

Gujarat

(i) Financial aid ought to be given from the very first year and not after three years to the minority institutions.

Karnataka

(i) The teachers were paid much less than what was shown in the acquittance roll. They got less than what they signed for.

(ii) Grants-in-aid were neither adequate nor timely.

(iii) The University Grants Commission was not releasing grants for some colleges.

(iv) The University Grants Commission's grants for Al - Hasnath College, Bangalore which was sanctioned in 1990 was not released to the college. Luqman College of Pharmacy, Gulbarga was not receiving any grants.

Kerala

(i) The maintenance grants at the rate of Rs. 5/- per student was quite inadequate.

(ii) Pay Commission's recommendations were not implemented.

(iii) Arrears were not paid for ten years to MES Manpad College, Kerala.

(iv) Adequate grants were not available for library, laboratory and building.

Maharashtra

(i) Inadequacy of grants and delay in the release of grants were the common grievances.

(ii) Non-salary grant as per formula was not sufficient.

(iii) Due to inflation, non-salary grants for sports activities were not sufficient.

(iv) Urdu High School Buldana did not receive any development and non-salary grants since 1972.

(v) No grants were given for first three years of recognition.

(vi) Only 25 per cent of the salary grant was paid after three years, and thereafter 25% increase was made every year.

(vii) No grants were given for pre-primary education.

Mizoram

(i) Grants-in-aid system adopted by the government was not prompt.

(ii) There was delay in the release of grants.

(iii) The teachers could not get their salary timely due to delay in the release of grants.

Orissa

(i) There was delay in the release of grants.

(ii) There was delay in the payment of salary.

Punjab

(i) Grants were not adequate.

(ii) There was delay in the release of grants.
(iii) The teachers were paid less than the prescribed scale.

Tamil Nadu

(i) There was delay in the release of grants for teachers on maternity leave/leave vacancy.
(ii) There was delay in sanctioning increments, arrears, loans, Provident Fund loans, pension and gratuity.
(iii) The release of grants was delayed.
(iv) The teacher who worked against permanent posts were not getting any allowance as long as their posts were not made permanent.
(v) There was acute shortage of funds for buildings.
(vi) No grants were given for furniture, equipments, library, sports and games, and audio-visual aids.
(vii) It was very difficult to get building structure and establishment certificate from Public Works Department.
(viii) Many orphanages in Tamil Nadu had not been recognized and had not been given any grants.
For those which received grant it was paid only at the end of the twelfth month.
(ix) To a school in Madras, the maintenance grants were not given since 1974, in spite of representations to the Directorate of Public Institution, and to the Secretary of the Department of Education.

Uttar Pradesh

(i) The minority institutions were facing difficulties due to lack of funds and they could not afford full facilities to the staff and students.
(ii) Since the students are exempted from paying fee by the government, there is an acute financial problem.
(iii) Development fee collected from the students was quite insufficient.
(iv) Schools find it difficult to provide furniture as there is no special grant given for the purpose.
(v) Building, furniture and science grants are not available to institutions.

(vi) The salary of the staff is usually delayed.

(vii) The salary grants, and dearness allowance arrears are always delayed.

West Bengal

(i) Very few monasteries in Darjeeling have been given any aid.

(ii) With almost no grants, or insufficient grants from the government, the monasteries cannot provide any meaningful facilities for education.

(iii) Grants were not regularly given.

(iv) Pay Commission's recommendations were not implemented due to insufficient funds.

(v) For students no facilities of scholarship, book grants, etc., exist.

Summary

On summing up the following common financial grievances come to the fore:

(i) Inadequacy of grants and funds;

(ii) Delay in release of grants;

(iii) No maintenance grant or inadequate maintenance grant;

(iv) Non-payment of government's pay-scale to teaching and non-teaching staff;

(v) No grant or very much negligible grant for building, equipments, library, laboratory, games and sports, and audio-visual aids;

(vi) Inadequate scholarship and book grants to students;

(vii) Pardah Nasheen school and Madrassa worst hit in terms of grants and funds;

(viii) Condition of Muslim and Buddhist managed institutions are worse in comparison with Christian, Parsi and Sikh managed educational institutions.

SEVEN

Conclusion: Outcome and Recommendations

The minority intellectuals and rich seemed to have failed the minority community. In fact, it continued to remain a rich and poor divide. The real interests of the poor and weak among the minorities generally had suffered.

This was more true of the Muslims and the Buddhists, than the Christians, the Parsis and the Sikhs. Education among Muslim women was greatly neglected. But the same did not apply in the Christians, or the Sikhs, or the Parsis. Among the Christians and the Sikhs, the women sometimes outnumbered men in the educational field.

Sometimes, it became very difficult to put grievances into separate and fixed categories, such as, financial and non-financial. In fact, they, at times, overlapped. Financial grievances were more critical. They often gave rise to the non-financial grievances as well; or non-financial grievances took their origin from the financial roots.

Once the cause of grievances of various minority managed educational institutions became known, it could be possible to remove these causes, and thereby, reduce the level of grievances. Inadequacy of funds to the institutions; delay in the release of grants by the state governments; and the paucity of funds on the part of the state governments, were interrelated sources of grievances. Any attempt to remove these grievances must take note of these interrelated areas of grievances.

It must be, therefore, seen that

(i) adequate or at least reasonably adequate grants were made available to these institutions;

(ii) the grants given by the state governments were released in time for which the state machinery had to be made efficient and also accountable;

(iii) the budget allocation in the area of education must increase in order to remove the difficulty on account of paucity of funding.

Inadequacy of grants to the institutions, and the paucity of funds on the part of the government were connected with overall position of funding in the area of education. The chronic underfunding of education, and regional and rural-urban disparities in educational outlays should be remedied by increasing government educational expenditures from 3.4% of G.D.P. in 1986-87, to, at least, 6.0% of G.D.P. in the current year as envisaged by the newly formed BJP-led government in the Centre.

No doubt, educational expenditures grew more rapidly in the 1980s than in previous decades. But this increased funding was, perhaps, not used to upgrade the existing facilities. The expenditure increases might have been used to raise pay allowances of the teaching staff. Only increase in educational funding is not enough. The increased educational funding should also be seen to be used to upgrade the existing facilities in educational institutions. This necessitated a change at the policy level. However, the delay in the release of grants was caused on account of the cumbersome administrative procedures, negligence in dealing on the part of the concerned dealing departments, and dealing hands, and corrupt practices often prevailing at these levels. This area of grievance related to the rules, procedures, and styles of functioning where the government machinery and functionaries were involved. This level must be made accountable, and efficient by regular monitoring, and supervision from the higher level functionaries. Unless this level was made effective and efficient, adequacy of funding in the area of education just might not be able to remove the grievances. At the same time, effective utilization of grants by the institutions had to be ensured. We should frankly admit that we had no way to judge whether effective utilization of grants was done at the level of these minority managed educational institutions.

All the same, the minority managed educational institutions should be encouraged to raise their own resources, and generate their own funds as far as possible. The rich and resourceful, particularly, among the Muslims should come forward and donate liberally to the cause of educational development among the Muslims. A portion of their donation to the religious organizations could go to the support of the educational institutions.

The gap between the perception of the government machinery, and the perception of the people in the management of minority managed educational institutions regarding the 'right to establish and administer educational institutions of their choice' also created scope for grievances. The Supreme Court, and the various High Courts, in their judicial pronouncements had allowed restrictions by way of regulation for the purpose of maintaining standards in minority managed educational institutions. The government officials would go by this consideration, and act under these guidelines, although there was always a scope for their discretion being used in the correct spirit of the court orders, and provisions of the Constitution.

The management of the minority institutions looked upon any move by the government authorities as interference over their rights to establish and administer institutions of their choice. This gap in their perception resulted in major grievances among the minority institutions, particularly those managed by the Muslims.

Most of these institutions were not properly staffed, their pay and other benefits, service conditions were not according to the rules and regulations. Naturally, they could not meet the requirement of maintaining educational standards. The institutions looked upon the government as the sole source of support in finance, and also other matters; teachers grumbled; students suffered; naturally, the government authorities found occasion to interfere. The management of the minority institutions considered it as encroachment on their right. They threw the blame on the shoulder of the government. This was the main cause of grievance of most institutions managed by the Muslim minority. These institutions had very few competent and dedicated teachers, had almost no element of competitiveness, and the general conditions were not so good; sometimes, some of the interested groups and people under the pretext of constitutional provisions, set up educational institutions, and used them as means to serve their own end rather than the goal of providing good education to their people. They did not hesitate to maladminister.

Effectiveness of Minorities Commission

The effective functioning of the Minorities Commission was likely to have its bearing upon the effective and efficient functioning of the minority educational institutions. In several states, the Minorities Commission/Minorities Welfare Board is non-existent. In some states where such Commission/Board existed, the position of Chairman/Vice-Chairman remained vacant. They were virtually non-functional and ineffective.

The staff was generally drafted from other government organizations, no specific staff was there to deal with the affairs of the minority managed educational institutions.

Some State Minorities Commissions alleged that they had no power to recruit staff. With present statutory status to the Minorities Commission in the centre, and if similar status were given to state minorities commissions, things might possibly look up.

The Minorities Commissions at the state level functioned more or less like a state department, and not as an independent, autonomous body. Minorities Commissions at various levels would have to be an effective instrument in securing development of minorities, especially, in the field of education.

Financial Corporation

The major grievance of the minority managed educational institutions arose from the inadequacy of grants and funds, and delay in their release. Their main sources of funds were government grants-in-aid, collection from students, public donation, in some cases, some external agencies. But, funds always remained their major area of grievance. Some agency (Central/State) like Financial Corporation might be created to give financial assistance, and also loans, in various forms, to the minority managed educational institutions, for their development and maintenance. This was needed more to give boost to science, technical, professional and vocational education among the backward lots among the minorities.

One-Time Equipment Grant after Every Five Years

The minority managed educational institutions were greatly handicapped on account of lack of teaching aids, audio-visual aids and equipments. The Minorities Commissions (at the Centre and State levels) were required to identify all such minority managed institutions which did not have adequate teaching aids and equipments, and they might be given one-time equipment grant; and the position could be reviewed after every five years. Such grants might be given more in terms of kind rather than cash.

Grievances Redressal Machinery

Grievances of the minority managed educational institutions were accumulating resulting in deterioration of educational standards in case of the economically and educationally more backward groups, like the Muslims and the Buddhists. To look into and bring an end to various types of grievances, particularly those relating to service conditions, salary, etc., of the staff, Grievances Redressal Machinery might be set up to function within the purview of the Minorities Commission in the Centre and at the State level, as the case might be.

Regionwise and Groupwise Micro-level Studies to have an In-depth View

The five religious minorities, the Buddhists, the Muslims, the Christians, the Parsis, and the Sikhs are differently placed in terms of their economic and educational development. Similarly, the situation is not the same in various regions. The Micro-level indepth studies of grievances of the minority managed educational institutions, regionwise as well as minority groupwise, should be made in order to have an indepth view of the problem.

Identifying the Region

Central-West-Southern Region

To start with:

(a) *Uttar Pradesh:* Uttar Pradesh is one of the biggest states, the state has cases pending for recognition since long (in many cases more than 10 years).

(b) *Bihar*: Bihar is largely neglected in education among the minorities, especially girls' education.

(c) *Maharashtra*: Maharashtra needs attention because of neo-Buddhists (who are generally converts from scheduled castes), and Parsi (who are on decline) populations.

(d) *Karnataka*: Karnataka has a number of Minority Organizations which run institutions of various types, charge high capitation fee, pay low salary to the staff, also face problem of interregional student intake.

North-Eastern Region

Important because of their geographical location, strategic situation, their Christian, Muslim and Buddhist populations are to be studied in particular.

Northern Region

(a) *Jammu & Kashmir*: J & K because of their predominantly Muslim and Buddhist population, and strategic situation.

(b) *Punjab*: Punjab because of its predominantly Sikh population, and strategic situation.

Identifying the group, according to priority as below:

(i) Buddhists
(ii) Muslims
(iii) Parsis
(iv) Christians (denominationwise)
(v) Sikhs

Case of the Buddhists: Do they Need Attention?

Much like the Muslims, the Buddhists too were economically and educationally backward. Grants given to the Buddhist institutions were very inadequate. There was not much financial problem in the urban area, the real problem lay in the rural area. Grants should be given regularly. In urban areas, the scholarships were given, but not in the rural area.

(i) Since Buddhist monastery was a free religious institution depending upon the public contribution, the government should come forward to assist this institution with grants-in-aid.

(ii) On asking whether the Pay Commission's recommendations were being implemented? 'The question did not arise'.

(iii) For students, no facilities of scholarship, book grants, etc., existed.

(iv) In Himachal Pradesh, in Lahaul-Spiti and Kinnaur regions, primary education was being imparted in Buddhist educational institutions. For higher education, the students were sent out to the Buddhist institutions in Uttar Pradesh and Karnataka.

There was need of institutions of higher education for the Buddhists there.

Formula of Grants: Need for Change

The formula enunciated by the state governments for the sanction of grants-in-aid did not suit the economically and educationally backward Minority Communities. The formula should be reasonably modified.

The proportion of allocation on scholarship, and particularly, pre-matric scholarship, based on economic criteria especially for women and children, should be increased.

The criteria of eligibility for scholarship for collegiate or technical studies, or for coaching facilities to prepare for various competitive examinations, or, for admission in technical institutions, should be family income from all sources to the extent of Rs. 30,000 per annum per family of five.

Untimely Release of Grants

The untimely release of grants caused much inconvenience to the Managing Committee, and dissatisfaction and frustration among the teaching and non-teaching staff. To mitigate this, grants should be released timely, preferably in three instalments:

(a) before the beginning of the academic session;

(b) after three months of the beginning of the session;

(c) and after eight months of the beginning of the session.

Training to Ulemas

There was no facility for Arabic scholars (Ulemas) to get teacher's training, because of which, they did not get the benefit of trained teachers' pay-scales. Training facility on state or regional basis may be provided for them.

Lack of Facilities

The minority managed educational institutions were placed at a disadvantageous position in regard to the availability of proper teaching aids, textbooks in Urdu, documentaries on education in Urdu and library and laboratory facilities. Main reasons behind these handicaps were the lack of adequate funds and lack of proper attention on the part of the state government.

The students, studying in minority educational institutions having poor facilities, suffered from several inadequacies. They had little facility for outdoor games; furniture was not properly made available, the low-paid teaching staff took little interest in improving the students' standard of education.

Discrimination and Deprivation

Muslim minority institutions alleged discrimination of two types:

(a) abnormal delay in grants-in-aid, and
(b) emoluments unequal to those given in the general government schools.

The government rules in this regard were violated by most institutions. This situation called for an immediate remedy.

Suggestions

Separate Grants: in Kind or Cash

Instead of giving lumpsum amount as maintenance grants, separate grants could be given for:

(a) teaching aids
(b) sports and games
(c) library
(d) maintenance

On the basis of actual expenditure, some of these grants should be given more in kind rather than cash.

Half of these grants should be released at the beginning of the academic year, and the rest immediately after submission of the final bills.

Time Limit for all Grants

Delay in the release of grants should be avoided by fixing a time limit for all official processes.

Special Case for Girls' Education

Pardah Nasheen schools which served the cause of girls' education among the Muslims should be given due financial support from the government as well as the community. The fate of girls' education was extremely deplorable. Social, educational and economic backwardness of the community could be greatly mitigated by taking due care of the girls' education among the Muslims, and also the Buddhists. In fact, the problem of educational backwardness among the Buddhist converts from scheduled castes, and the Muslim, has assumed a serious proportion, and deserved quick attention at the highest level.

To Prevent Drop outs

To prevent drop outs among the children, support through scholarships, and other benefits, like arrangement of midday meals at the primary stage, as in Tamil Nadu to attract children, appeared to be necessary. Some of the respondents mentioned that if the poor Muslim boys received education up to secondary level, they could not remain a burden on the society; they could be self-sustaining.

Grants-in-aid without Regulation

As far as possible, every minority managed educational institution should be encouraged to generate its own fund; government aid should be treated as a blessing in disguise. It should be treated as supportive and supplementary because government aid also led to unnecessary interference. It would not be wise to say "give us money and leave things to our own discretion". The agency, which would give aid, would tend to bring in pressure and regulation of some kind. Some regulation and control would be an inescapable precondition for any grants-in-aid. A World Bank study (India: Poverty, Employment, and Social Services), says, "roughly 60 per cent of school funds are allocated as grants to aided institutions over which, apart from occasional and perfunctory inspections, state authorities have little control. These schools may be absorbing funding increases without providing additional services. There appears to be a need to increase accountability and control over how money is spent".

Recommendations

The Case of the Parsis: Flexibility in Rules Needed

The problem of the Parsis was different. It was more social and cultural rather than educational. The Zoroastrians were, no doubt a minority managed educational society, but since their own number of students was extremely depleted they could not conduct a school giving preference to their own language. Therefore, they conducted English medium schools for the benefit of all communities. This became the reason for their not receiving grants-in-aid. On the ground of medium of instruction (if it is other than mother tongue), grants-in-aid should not be denied.

One such school in Pune, Roshni High School, was a top ranking school in academics and physical education. In S.S.C. Examinations they had achieved excellent results from 90% to 100%. Their students had been selected for the basket ball team to represent the district at the state level. After standard IV, the students of this school join other schools in the vicinity, which receive grants-in-aid and charge no fee. Naturally, the divisions of this school get depleted, only one division remains; and students of poor calibre remain. The rules of the government thus have a both quantitatively and qualitatively adverse effect.

In spite of all their efforts they were not given financial assistance by the government in the form of grants-in-aid. They had to depend upon their own collections of fees and donations for fund. They could not pay their teachers the rising government scales and other allowances. Naturally, on the one hand their staff was dissatisfied; on the other hand, the parents were getting burdened with payment of increasing fees.

Rules relating to the grants-in-aid should be made so flexible as to take due care of such cases of minority educational institutions.

Rules should be promotive rather than restrictive because the ultimate purpose is achievement of academic excellence and standards, and, not sheer enforcement of rules for rules' sake.

There should be imaginative interpretation of rules with some amount of flexibility to help the cause of educational institutions managed by the minorities.

Integrated Educational Development Programme (IEDP)

The high power panel on minorities (constituted by the Ministry of Home Affairs, Government of India, in their report 1993), suggested introduction of a central scheme, like, the Integrated Educational Development Programme (IEDP) for the weak among the minorities. This scheme which could be run by the Ministry of Welfare, with funding from the Planning Commission, should be introduced, at the earliest, for the educational development among the minorities.

PART III

NON-FINANCIAL and OTHER GRIEVANCES

EIGHT

Non-Financial Grievances of the Minority Managed Educational Institutions

The non-financial and other grievances of the minority managed educational institutions are numerous. If the finances of these institutions are weak, naturally the various types of facilities of modern education would not be available to them. Inadequacy of furniture for teaching and non-teaching staff, and students; inadequacy of library, teaching aids, games and sports, hostel, and other facilities, were the common causes of grievance. The poor service conditions, lack of promotional avenues, lack of incentives, lack of health and housing facilities; inadequacy of teaching and training facilities, marked most of these institutions.

Apathy and indifference of parents, apathy of students, especially in Muslim schools, created a discouraging atmosphere. Poverty and illiteracy among these groups were greatly responsible for a deplorable condition of education among them.

Sometimes, bickerings and inner conflicts in management; between teachers; between teachers and head of the institutions, vitiated the educational environment. Institutions having little extracurricular activities, almost no laboratory facilities and audio-visual aids, presented a hopeless situation. Numerous institutions without facilities of toilets, or separate toilets for boys and girls, poor drinking water facilities were usual.

In rural areas, school facilities had not yet been provided within a walking distance to a good number of these minorities. In villages, classes were conducted in cow-sheds, or under the shade of a tree, etc., with a single teacher. Parents prefer to send their children to work in the field. Even in urban area, there were neither proper buildings nor equipments, such a situation prevails even today. Drop outs among students, and truancy among teachers particularly, in the rural areas in primary schools, are the symptoms of the disease.

An analysis of the state wise situation of grievances is presented in Tables 8.1 to 8.8 given at the end of this chapter.

Adequacy of Furniture

(i) For Students and Teachers

According to the perception of heads of institutions, in majority of the institutions in Andhra Pradesh, Bihar, Delhi, Gujarat, Karnataka, Kerala, Punjab, and in all institutions in Chandigarh and Haryana, the furniture for students and teachers were totally adequate.

All the institutions in Mizoram, Orissa and West Bengal one-third in Andhra Pradesh, five-tenths in Maharashtra and Uttar Pradesh had accepted that the furniture for students and teachers were inadequate.

(ii) For Non-Teaching Staff

Large proportions of these institutions in various states also had reported that the furniture for non-teaching staff was totally adequate, while about one-fourth of all institutions in various states had reported that they were inadequate.

Two-thirds of institutions in Mizoram, one-third in Andhra Pradesh, one-fourth in Karnataka and one-tenth in Uttar Pradesh had accepted they were "not at all existing" (Table 8.1).

Adequacy of Infrastructure

(i) Library (ii) Laboratory (iii) Teaching aids

All the institutions in Chandigarh and Haryana, two-thirds of institutions in Andhra Pradesh, three-fourths in Bihar affirm that the library, laboratory facilities and teaching aids were totally adequate in their institutions. Another one-fourth of institutions in Bihar reported that they were inadequate, while one-third in Andhra Pradesh has reported either "inadequate" or "not at all existing".

All the institutions in Mizoram, Maharashtra, Orissa, and Punjab, and larger proportion in Maharashtra reported that these facilities were either "inadequate" or not "at all existing".

(iv) Adequacy of facilities for sports and games and hostel

The hostel facilities did not exist in any of the institutions in Delhi, Gujarat and Haryana; for majority of the institutions in Andhra Pradesh, Karnataka, Punjab and West Bengal; and for majority of the institutions in Bihar and Kerala; and slightly less than half in Tamil Nadu and Uttar Pradesh; the hostel facilities were not available to the students.

In more than half of the institutions in Punjab, Uttar Pradesh, Maharashtra and all the institutions in Orissa, Punjab and West Bengal sports and games were either "inadequate" or "not at all existing". This is also true for half the institutions studied in Delhi, Tamil Nadu and Karnataka (Table 8.2).

Grievances of Teaching Staff

Pay

The delay in payment of salary occurs in all the institutions of Bihar, half of the institutions in Andhra Pradesh and Delhi, merely one-third of the institutions in Orissa and Maharashtra and four-tenths of the institutions in Uttar Pradesh.

In states like Gujarat, Punjab and Tamil Nadu, in as much as between one-tenth to one-fifth of the institutions payment was delayed for teaching staff. (Table 8.3)

Payment of allowances

Very few states like Andhra Pradesh, Chandigarh and Tamil Nadu where between one-fourth to one-third of institutions did not pay the allowances to teaching staff.

Lack of promotional avenue and others

The sample teachers in all the institutions studied in Delhi, West Bengal and in Orissa, two-thirds in Mizoram and Tamil Nadu, two-fourths in Bihar, Kerala and Maharashtra, one-third in Andhra Pradesh and Gujarat had revealed that one of their main grievances was lack of promotional avenues. It is also to be observed that in considerable proportion, the teaching staff of the institutions in these states did not agree with their colleagues.

This trend persisted for lack of incentives too as a grievance. The teaching staff of these institutions were divided over this issue though proportion in either side was of much importance. This is also true of lack of health and educational facilities, and lack of training/teaching facilities (Table 8.3).

Attitude of Management, Head of Institution, Colleagues and Non-Teaching Staff

The teaching staff consulted in most of the institutions in various states did not have much against the management whose attitude they felt was encouraging. The exception in large proportion of the institutions being in states, such as, Chandigarh and Mizoram where the teaching staff felt that the management was either "not encouraging" or "discouraging". This trend is exhibited for the attitude of head of institution, colleagues and non-teaching staff too.

Mizoram being the exception in all cases, where all institutions reported that the attitude of all these persons was not encouraging to the teaching staff (Table 8.4).

Attitude of Students, Parents and Government Authorities

The attitude of students was encouraging; was the reply of teaching staff in all the institutions in Gujarat, Haryana, Orissa and Punjab, while it was so in most of the institutions in Andhra Pradesh, Bihar, Karnataka, Maharashtra and Uttar Pradesh.

More or less half of the institutions in Tamil Nadu, and Kerala, and all, in Mizoram reported that they were "not encouraging". Four-fifths of institutions in Chandigarh and Delhi reported that they were either "not encouraging" or "discouraging".

The trend on attitude of parents was less impressive than it is on students. Perhaps, teaching staff who may forgive students for their ignorance may not let the parents go out of responsibility, and the general trend among them about the parents of minority community children was that they are indifferent to the problems of their children.

The government authorities did not command good opinion from teaching staff as the Table 8.5 shows that in most of the states, in more than half of the institutions, teaching staff feel that the government authorities are either 'not encouraging' or 'discouraging'.

Lack of Motivation of Students

Almost in all states, exceptions being Gujarat and Mizoram most of the teaching staff consulted had reported that weak financial conditions of students was the main reason to the lack of motivation.

In Andhra Pradesh, in the perception of majority of the teaching staff, weak financial conditions of students, inadequate facilities of the school, poor opportunities for higher education and employment are the reasons to a large extent for the lack of motivation. The same reasons were quoted either as 'to a large extent' or 'to some extent' in more than two-fourths of the institutions in Chandigarh, Delhi, Kerala, Maharashtra, Mizoram, Orissa, Tamil Nadu, Uttar Pradesh and West Bengal.

Unimpressive curriculum was quoted in many states while unimpressive teaching was less quoted as a reason to some extent for the lack of motivation (Table 8.6).

Evaluation of Students about the Institutions

Table 8.7 shows the opinion of students on various aspects of their institutions. Though the condition of one institution cannot be generalized to another, an effort is made here to find out how minority institutions in different places perform their function in the educational development of minorities.

As far as teaching and studies were concerned, very few proportion of institutions in any state had been rated as 'excellent' by students. The students of all institutions in Mizoram, Orissa, Haryana and West Bengal had rated them as 'good', while none of the institutions in any state were rated as "not at all good", one-third of institutions in Bihar and Tamil Nadu; and one-fourth in Kerala had been rated as "not so good".

The library and reading materials were "excellent" in nearly three-fourths of institutions in Karnataka, while in all the institutions in Gujarat and Haryana; and majority of institutions in Andhra Pradesh and Punjab they were "good".

In half of the institutions in Chandigarh and in two-thirds of institutions in West Bengal they were "not at all good"; while in all the institutions in Bihar, Mizoram and Orissa they were not so good.

The students of the majority of the institutions in Chandigarh, Delhi, Gujarat, Haryana, Karnataka and Orissa felt that the class-room was good in their opinion.

The students of half of the institutions in Punjab, Mizoram, two-thirds of Bihar, and four-tenths of Uttar Pradesh had stated that they were 'not so good'.

As far as games and sports were concerned, the students of larger proportion of institutions in Chandigarh, Gujarat, Haryana, Kerala, and Punjab, reported that they were good in their institutions, whereas the students of larger proportions in Bihar, Delhi, Karnataka, Maharashtra, Orissa, Uttar Pradesh and West Bengal had either said as "not so good" or "not at all good".

The extracurricular activities more or less followed similar pattern in these states.

Evaluation of Students about the Institute

The laboratory was good in all the institutions in Haryana; while it was so in three-fifths of institutions studied in Gujarat, Punjab, and half of the institutions in Uttar Pradesh. In greater proportions of institutions' students had reported that as either "not so good" or "not at all good". The laboratory facilities, notably, were nil in half of the institutions in Mizoram, and two-thirds of institutions in West Bengal (Table 8.8).

The toilet facilities, the students of all institutions in Haryana had reported were 'excellent' while majority of the students in Gujarat, Karnataka and Mizoram had reported that they were 'good'.

However, in larger proportions of institutions of Bihar, Chandigarh, Delhi, Orissa, Punjab, Tamil Nadu, Uttar Pradesh and West Bengal they were 'either not so good' or 'nil'. Half of the institutions in Mizoram reported the toilet facility as 'nil'.

As a matter of fact, the non-financial grievances arise from the financial causes. Weak finances, apathy of the governmental authorities, coupled with poor response of the community have created conditions for multiple grievances of the minority managed educational institutions. No doubt, the levels of these grievances vary from region to region, group to group, and institution to institution. They take numerous shapes in different types of institutions managed by the minorities.

In some cases, the grievance is on account of recognition or affiliation; in other cases, it is on account of recruitment, promotion, teaching and reading facilities, and sundry other small matters. The point is that the gravity of the situation must be understood and appreciated in order to remedy it.

TABLE - 8.1
PERCENTAGE DISTRIBUTION OF OPINION OF HEAD OF INSTITUTION ON ADEQUACY OF FURNITURES

Sl. No.	State/U.T.	*For Students*			*For Teachers*			*For Non-Teaching Staff*		
		Totally Adequate	*Inade-quate*	*Not at all Existing*	*Totally Adequate*	*Inade-quate*	*Not at all Existing*	*Totally Adequate*	*Inade-quate*	*Not at all Existing*
1.	Andhra Pradesh	67	33	-	67	33	-	50	17	33
2.	Bihar	75	25	-	75	25	-	75	25	-
3.	Chandigarh	100	-	-	100	-	-	100	-	-
4.	Delhi	75	25	-	100	-	-	100	-	-
5.	Gujarat	83	17	-	100	-	-	83	17	-
6.	Haryana	100	-	-	100	-	-	100	-	-
7.	Karnataka	72	28	-	72	28	-	50	28	22
8.	Kerala	70	30	-	70	30	-	60	40	-
9.	Maharashtra	44	56	-	50	50	-	31	63	6
10.	Mizoram	-	100	-	-	100	-	-	33	67
11.	Orissa	-	100	-	-	100	-	44	56	-
12.	Punjab	63	37	-	63	37	-	63	37	-
13.	Tamil Nadu	42	50	8	67	33	-	50	42	8
14.	Uttar Pradesh	33	56	11	44	44	12	67	22	11
15.	West Bengal	-	100	-	-	100	-	-	100	-

TABLE - 8.2

PERCENTAGE DISTRIBUTION OF OPINION OF HEAD OF INSTITUTION OF ADEQUACY OF IMPORTANT INFRASTRUCTURES AT THEIR INSTITUTIONS

Sl. No.	State/U.T.	Library			Laboratory			Teaching Aids			Sports and Games			Hostel		
		Totally Adequate	Inadequate	Not at all Existing	Totally Adequate	Inadequate	Not at all Existing	Totally Adequate	Inadequate	Not at all Existing	Totally Adequate	Inadequate	Not at all Existing	Totally Adequate	Inadequate	Not at all Existing
1.	Andhra Pradesh	67	17	16	67	17	16	67	17	16	67	17	16	-	17	83
2.	Bihar	75	25	-	75	25	-	75	25	-	75	25	-	-	50	50
3.	Chandigarh	100	-	-	100	-	-	100	-	-	100	-	-	-	100	-
4.	Delhi	50	50	-	75	25	-	50	50	-	50	50	-	-	-	100
5.	Gujarat	67	33	-	83	17	-	83	17	-	83	17	-	-	-	100
6.	Haryana	100	-	-	100	-	-	100	-	-	100	-	-	-	-	100
7.	Karnataka	50	50	-	33	39	28	61	33	6	56	44	-	11	-	89
8.	Kerala	80	20	-	50	50	-	50	40	10	40	60	-	20	30	50
9.	Maharashtra	31	63	6	25	31	44	19	69	12	19	63	18	6	69	25
10.	Mizoram	-	75	25	-	75	25	-	100	-	-	100	-	-	75	25
11.	Orissa	-	100	-	-	75	25	-	100	-	-	100	-	-	100	-
12.	Punjab	-	37	63	-	37	63	50	50	-	25	75	-	25	12	63
13.	Tamil Nadu	58	33	9	50	17	33	66	25	9	50	33	17	25	33	42
14.	Uttar Pradesh	67	22	11	44	44	12	56	33	11	44	44	12	12	44	44
15.	West Bengal	-	-	100	-	-	100	-	-	100	-	100	-	-	33	67

TABLE - 8.3

PERCENTAGE DISTRIBUTION OF NON-FINANCIAL GRIEVANCES OF TEACHING STAFF

Sl. No.	State/U.T.	Grievances on Pay						Service Conditions							
		Delay in Pay		*Less than Prescribed Scale*		*No Payment of Allowances*		*Lack of Promotional Avenue*		*Lack of Incentives*		*No Housing/ Health/ Educational Facilities*		*Lack of Teaching/Training Library Facilities*	
		Yes	*No*	*Yes*	*No*	*Yes*	*No*	*Yes*	*No*	*Yes*	*No*	*Yes*	*No*	*Yes*	*No*
1.	Andhra Pradesh	50	50	33	67	33	67	33	67	33	67	33	67	33	67
2.	Bihar	100	-	-	100	-	100	50	50	75	25	50	50	50	50
3.	Chandigarh	-	100	25	75	25	75	100	-	100	-	100	-	75	25
4.	Delhi	56	44	11	89	-	100	44	66	100	-	78	22	56	44
5.	Gujarat	17	83	-	100	-	100	33	67	-	100	-	100	-	100
6.	Haryana	-	100	-	100	-	100	-	100	-	100	100	-	-	100
7.	Karnataka	6	94	11	89	11	89	17	83	17	83	17	83	11	89
8.	Kerala	9	91	9	91	-	100	50	50	50	50	100	100	82	18
9.	Maharashtra	31	69	25	75	-	100	50	50	50	50	73	37	19	81
10.	Mizoram	-	-	33	67	-	-	67	33	-	100	33	67	33	67
11.	Orissa	33	67	-	100	-	100	100	-	67	33	67	33	67	33
12.	Punjab	13	87	-	100	13	87	13	87	50	50	38	62	13	87
13.	Tamil Nadu	17	83	33	67	33	67	67	33	58	42	75	25	50	50
14.	Uttar Pradesh	44	66	-	100	11	89	22	78	56	44	44	56	44	56
15.	West Bengal	-	100	-	100	-	100	67	33	33	56	33	67	33	67

TABLE - 8.4

PERCENTAGE DISTRIBUTION OF OPINION OF TEACHING STAFF ON ATTITUDE OF MANAGEMENT, HEAD OF INSTITUTION, COLLEAGUES AND NON-TEACHING STAFF

Sl. No.	State/U.T.	*Management*			*Head of Institution*			*Colleagues*			*Non-Teaching Staff*		
		Encouraging	*Not Encouraging*	*Discouraging*	*Encouraging*	*Not Encouraging*	*Discouraging*	*Encouraging*	*Not Encouraging*	*Discouraging*	*Encouraging*	*Not Encouraging*	*Discouraging*
1.	Andhra Pradesh	60	20	20	80	-	20	80	-	20	57	-	42
2.	Bihar	100	-	-	100	-	-	100	-	-	100	-	-
3.	Chandigarh	20	60	20	40	20	40	40	40	20	40	20	40
4.	Delhi	60	10	30	100	-	-	82	18	-	45	36	19
5.	Gujarat	100	-	-	100	-	-	100	-	-	100	-	-
6.	Haryana	100	-	-	100	-	-	100	-	-	100	-	-
7.	Karnataka	81	6	13	94	6	-	100	-	-	94	6	-
8.	Kerala	75	19	6	94	6	-	94	6	-	82	18	-
9.	Maharashtra	93	7	-	100	-	-	85	15	-	86	14	-
10.	Mizoram	-	100	-	-	100	-	-	100	-	-	100	-
11.	Orissa	-	-	-	100	-	-	100	-	-	100	-	-
12.	Punjab	88	12	-	75	25	-	88	12	-	88	12	-
13.	Tamil Nadu	55	35	10	80	20	-	85	15	-	60	40	-
14.	Uttar Pradesh	100	-	-	100	-	-	100	-	-	100	-	-
15.	West Bengal	100	-	-	100	-	-	100	-	-	-	-	-

TABLE - 8.5

PERCENTAGE DISTRIBUTION OF TEACHING STAFF — THEIR OPINION ON ATTITUDE OF STUDENTS, PARENTS AND GOVERNMENT AUTHORITIES

Sl. No.	State/U.T.	*Students*			*Parents*			*Govt. Authorities*		
		Encouraging	*Not Encouraging*	*Discouraging*	*Encouraging*	*Not Encouraging*	*Discouraging*	*Encouraging*	*Not Encouraging*	*Discouraging*
1.	Andhra Pradesh	80	-	20	60	20	20	60	20	20
2.	Bihar	75	25	-	50	50	-	25	50	25
3.	Chandigarh	20	40	40	-	60	40	20	40	40
4.	Delhi	18	55	27	18	27	55	40	40	20
5.	Gujarat	100	-	-	80	20	-	80	20	-
6.	Haryana	100	-	-	100	-	-	100	-	-
7.	Karnataka	81	19	-	75	25	-	50	31	19
8.	Kerala	59	41	-	65	35	-	33	50	17
9.	Maharashtra	93	7	-	57	29	-	-	100	-
10.	Mizoram	-	100	-	-	100	-	-	100	-
11.	Orissa	100	-	-	33	67	-	33	67	-
12.	Punjab	100	-	-	100	-	-	63	37	-
13.	Tamil Nadu	50	45	-	50	45	5	-	87	13
14.	Uttar Pradesh	86	14	-	71	29	-	71	29	-
15.	West Bengal	-	-	-	-	-	-	-	-	100

TABLE - 8.6

PERCENTAGE DISTRIBUTION OF OPINION ON LACK OF MOTIVATION OF STUDENTS

Sl. No.	State/U.T.	*Unimpressive Teaching*			*Unimpressive Curriculum*			*Weak Financial Conditions of Students*			*Inadequate Facilities of School/College*			*Poor Opportunities for Higher Education*			*Poor Opportunities for Employment*		
		To a Large Extent	*To Some Extent*	*Not at All*	*To a Large Extent*	*To Some Extent*	*Not at All*	*To a Large Extent*	*To Some Extent*	*Not at All*	*To a Large Extent*	*To Some Extent*	*Not at All*	*To a Large Extent*	*To Some Extent*	*Not at All*	*To a Large Extent*	*To Some Extent*	*Not at All*
1.	Andhra Pradesh	60	20	20	50	25	25	80	-	20	80	-	20	80	-	20	60	20	20
2.	Bihar	-	25	75	-	50	50	25	75	-	25	25	50	25	50	25	75	25	-
3.	Chandigarh	100	-	-	100	-	-	50	50	-	-	100	-	50	50	-	100	-	-
4.	Delhi	-	43	57	43	57	-	60	40	-	18	64	18	63	13	24	33	44	23
5.	Gujarat	-	33	67	-	33	67	33	17	50	17	-	83	-	83	17	33	50	17
6.	Haryana	-	-	100	-	100	-	-	100	-	-	-	100	-	-	100	-	100	-
7.	Karnataka	36	14	50	43	7	50	38	31	31	43	7	50	38	13	49	44	25	31
8.	Kerala	-	47	53	20	60	20	75	25	-	47	33	20	33	20	47	47	33	20
9.	Maharashtra	18	47	35	29	53	18	69	19	12	40	33	27	53	33	14	71	18	11
10.	Mizoram	-	100	-	-	100	-	-	-	100	50	50	-	-	-	100	50	-	50
11.	Orissa	-	100	-	-	100	-	100	-	100	100	-	-	-	100	-	67	33	-
12.	Punjab	50	25	25	60	20	20	67	17	16	40	40	20	80	-	20	67	17	16
13.	Tamil Nadu	7	50	43	13	69	18	83	17	-	33	44	23	36	14	50	44	50	6
14.	Uttar Pradesh	-	50	50	20	30	30	57	43	-	50	33	17	17	66	17	83	17	-
15.	West Bengal	-	100	-	50	50	-	100	-	-	50	50	-	100	-	-	100	-	-

TABLE - 8.7
PERCENTAGE DISTRIBUTION OF EVALUATION BY STUDENTS ABOUT THE INSTITUTIONS

		Teaching and Studies			Library and Reading Materials				Classroom				Games and Sports					Extracurricular Activities			
Sl. No.	State/U.T.	Excellent	Good	Not so Good	Excellent	Good	Not so Good	Not at all Good	Excellent	Good	Not so Good	Not at all Good	Excellent	Good	Not so Good	Not at all Good	Nil	Excellent	Good	Not so Good	Not at all Good
1.	Andhra Pradesh	40	60	-	20	60	20	-	20	40	20	20	20	40	20	-	20	40	20	20	-
2.	Bihar	-	67	33	-	-	100	-	-	33	67	-	-	33	33	34	-	-	-	33	33
3.	Chandigarh	50	50	-	-	50	-	50	-	100	-	-	-	75	25	-	-	-	67	-	33
4.	Delhi	40	60	-	-	40	30	30	10	70	10	10	10	20	50	20	-	10	20	40	-
5.	Gujarat	20	80	-	-	100	-	-	-	80	20	-	-	60	40	-	-	-	40	60	-
6.	Haryana	-	100	-	-	100	-	-	-	100	-	-	-	100	-	-	-	-	100	-	-
7.	Karnataka	36	64	-	71	29	-	-	14	57	29	-	7	43	50	-	-	7	57	36	-
8.	Kerala	33	42	25	27	47	13	13	29	43	21	7	13	60	20	7	-	14	43	43	-
9.	Maharashtra	29	57	14	14	22	50	14	14	50	50	-	15	23	54	8	-	15	31	46	-
10.	Mizoram	-	100	-	-	-	100	-	-	50	50	-	-	50	50	-	-	-	50	50	-
11.	Orissa	-	100	-	-	-	100	-	-	67	33	-	-	-	100	-	-	-	-	100	-
12.	Punjab	13	74	13	13	79	13	-	-	50	50	-	-	63	37	-	-	14	71	15	-
13.	Tamil Nadu	21	42	37	26	42	11	21	21	26	21	32	16	32	37	5	20	32	21	16	5
14.	Uttar Pradesh	14	72	14	14	43	14	29	-	-	43	57	-	29	43	14	14	-	29	43	14
15.	West Bengal	-	100	-	-	33	-	67	-	-	33	67	-	-	100	-	-	-	100	-	-

TABLE - 8.8

PERCENTAGE DISTRIBUTION OF EVALUATION BY STUDENTS — ABOUT THE INSTITUTE

Sl. No.	State/U.T.	Laboratory					Toilet				
		Excellent	Good	Not so Good	Not at all Good	Nil	Excellent	Good	Not so Good	Not at all Good	Nil
1.	Andhra Pradesh	20	40	20	-	20	20	40	20	-	20
2.	Bihar	-	-	67	33	-	-	33	34	33	-
3.	Chandigarh	25	-	25	25	25	-	25	25	50	-
4.	Delhi	-	38	25	25	12	-	22	44	34	
5.	Gujarat	-	60	40	-	-	-	80	20	-	-
6.	Haryana	-	100	-	-	-	100	-	-	-	-
7.	Karnataka	8	33	33	-	26	25	58	17	-	-
8.	Kerala	14	43	7	7	29	13	47	20	20	-
9.	Maharashtra	15	23	31	8	23	17	25	42	8	-
10.	Mizoram	-	-	-	5	50	-	50	-	-	50
11.	Orissa	-	-	100	-	-	-	-	75	25	-
12.	Punjab	13	63	13	-	11	-	43	57	-	-
13.	Tamil Nadu	12	41	18	12	17	17	28	17	38	-
14.	Uttar Pradesh	-	50	16	17	17	17	33	17	33	-
15.	West Bengal	-	-	33	-	67	-	-	100	-	-

NINE

Minority Organizations and Institutions in the Field of Education: Some Case-Studies

Muslim Organizations and Institutions

(a) Journey from *Muflis, Lawaris* to well managed educational institutions: Anjuman Taalimul Muslemeen (Jaipur)

(b) Madina Educational Society (Hyderabad)

Christian Organizations

The Church of North India (Nagpur)

Parsi Organization and Institutions

The Bai Avabai Framji Petit Girl's Orphanage (Mumbai)

This chapter presents case-studies of some minority managed organizations and institutions in the field of education. Their managerial and leadership role, initiative, orientation towards the community, and the case of education, may be emulated as examples, by various other organizations and institutions. Their problems and grievances may have some common characteristics. Such organizations could be viewed as a model in the area of minorities' education which may have larger and long-term implications for the education among the minorities. *Sir Syed Group of Schools*, in Calcutta, are struggling, and yet making experiments in their own way, devoted to the cause of the minorities' education. They are running primary and junior high Schools on their own. They are now toying with the idea of 'Community College' to suit the educational needs of the community with an eye to economic necessities and compulsions.

Here, two Muslim organizations from Jaipur and Hyderabad; one Christian organization from Nagpur; and the other Parsi institution from Mumbai, have been presented as separate cases.

Journey from Muflis, Lawaris to well Managed Educational Institutions: A Case-Study of Anjuman Taalimul Muslemeen (Jaipur)

From a modest beginning of one single "Islami Madarsa" under the management of the then Islami Panchayati in 1926 to the present state of about a dozen educational institutions of all types under the management of Anjuman Taalimul Muslemeen is a long journey. This chapter presents an account of the journey of a Muslim organization in Jaipur (Rajasthan) known as Anjuman Taalimul Muslemeen now managing a number of educational institutions. This case-study, relates to a period of nearly two decades between 1967 and 1988; how a Muslim educational institution grew over a period of two decades under the care of its management. A brief background of the case is given here. Anjuman Taalimul Muslemeen was registered under Societies Registration Act 1860; it was further registered under Income Tax Registration Act 1962 for having exemption under 80-G; and also under Foreign Contribution Regulation Act 1976.

The educational institutions, particularly schools, under their management are duly recognized by the Department of Education, Government of Rajasthan.

The motto of this organization is,

"Education is as essential in Islam as spirit in a body".

The objective of Anjuman Taalimul Muslemeen is to spread and propagate education among the downtrodden Muslim community in Jaipur.

It has made pioneering effort in girls' education not only in Jaipur city but in the whole state of Rajasthan. There are now about 1900 girl students in the institutions run by them.

A little over two decades ago, the condition of Muslim schools (3) under Anjuman was rather poor academically, administratively and financially. Salaries of the staff were neither paid in time nor at the full rate. There was discontent and infighting among staff members. These institutions had no permanent source of income, except the grants-in-aid; meagre fees realized from students' and small donations collected on the eve of festivals like Idul-Fitr, Idul-Zuha. Teachers and students used to beg in front of mosques on the above occasions and on Friday. There were no classrooms but only open barracks without concrete floor, furniture and light. Basic minimum facilities of toilets, urinals, etc., did not exist.

The Muslim secondary school campus was completely exposed on the eastern side, making it a place of night shelter for animals.

The other two schools (Muslim Boys' Primary School and Muslim Girls' Primary School) were housed in rented buildings and their condition was not good. The academic state was far from satisfactory. The strength of students was approximately 650. The percentage result was discouraging. The administrative machinery was at a standstill. The credit of these institutions was at the lowest ebb. A sense of insecurity prevailed among the staff; a number of them left in disgust opting out for even lower positions elsewhere.

Looking at the condition then, schools were nicknamed as 'Muflis and Lawaris Schools'.

The present management took over the responsibility of these seriously ailing institutions at this critical juncture. The immediate task before them was to improve the shattered economy and poor image of these institutions for which sustained efforts were needed.

Now, as they say, the days of mid-sixties, academically, administratively and financially are gone.

If we look at the situation today as compared to that in 1967, there is a sea change (in both quantity and quality) in the position during 1967 and 1989 as far as the educational institutions managed by the Anjuman Society are concerned. Tables 9.1 and 9.2 give the comparative change in institutions managed by Anjuman Society.

Besides, the Anjuman is also guiding *Mohalla*-wise primary-cum-Madarsa institutions.

The facilities, such as, laboratories, big size classrooms, hall, open courtyard, library and reading room, craft room and toilets are also available.

TABLE - 9.1
INSTITUTIONS UNDER ANJUMAN SOCIETY POSITION: 1967 AND 1988

Position of institutions in 1967	1988
Name and number of institutions:	
(i) Muslim Boys' Primary School	(i) Muslim Boys' Primary School
(ii) Muslim Girls' Primary School	(ii) Muslim Girls' Primary School
(iii) Muslim Secondary School	(iii) Muslim Model Primary School (Coeducational)
	(iv) Muslim Girls' Middle School
	(v) Muslim Girls' Senior Higher Secondary School
	(vi) Muslim Senior Higher Secondary School
Technical Institution	
Nil	Muslim Women Industrial Training Institute (I) (Recognized by the government)
Non-formal Institution	
Nil	(i) Adult Literacy Centre
	(ii) Coaching and Training Centre
	(iii) Socio-Economic Centre
	(iv) Research and Survey Bureau

Source: *Parvaz-E-Anjuman* (Souvenir - Muslim Schools), March 1989, Jaipur

Now the Anjuman has a fairly good source of income from its , 95 shops, a bank building, book and stationery store and a substantial amount of donation collected every year by management without involving the staff and the students.

Results have gone up to 90 per cent. Its two campuses on Moti Doongri Road and Geejgarh House are continuously developing.

The Central Wakf Council gave them 50 per cent matching grants, that is, Rs. 75,000 (the first grant of its kind in Rajasthan) for Women Industrial Training Institute.

Some new projects have been completed.

Science laboratories with a cost of rupees six lakh fifty thousand, and computer project at a cost of one lakh fifty thousand have been completed.

Other new projects, like Auditorium-cum-Community Centre,

Boys' Hostel, etc., have been envisaged at a cost of twenty lakh rupees raised by public donation.

There are some projects in hand for girls' education, such as, Muslim Girls' Hostel, Muslim B.Ed College, Muslim Women Polytechnic, at a cost of rupees thirty lakhs, and assisted by Islamic Development Bank, Jeddah, Saudi Arabia.

TABLE - 9.2
INSTITUTIONS UNDER ANJUMAN SOCIETY POSITION: 1967 AND 1988

Sl. No.	*Particulars*	*Year*	
		1967	*1988*
1.	Strength of Students (boys and girls)	650	3600
2.	Sanctioned Strength of Staff	36	70
3.	Total Strength of Staff	36	150
4.	Salary	Rs. 90,000 (1966-67)	Rs. 16,00,000 (1988-89)
5.	Grants-in-Aid	Rs. 52,415 (1966-67)	Rs. 6,28,393 (1987-88)
6.	Expenditure on Construction	Almost nil	Approximately 2 lakhs (annually on an average)
7.	Provident Fund during the year	Rs. 2700	Rs. 85,000
8.	Amount of Fixed Deposit	Nil	Rs. 1,47,000
9.	Source of Income	Donations (very nominal)	(i) Donations (ii) Income from rentals
10.	Building Accommodation	20 rooms (barrack type) at M.D. Road	38 rooms (old and new) 100 rooms (at Geejgarh House)
11.	Books in Library	4311	11,600
12.	Books and Stationery Store	Nil	With revolving capital of Rs. 4 lakhs
13.	Garden and Lawn	Nil	Spacious Lawns and Garden
14.	Commercial Complex	Nil	(i) 95 Shops (ii) Bank Building
15.	Furniture and Equipments (Value in Rs.)	Not known	Rs. 3,25,000 (approx.)

The Anjuman Society is now recognized as one of the front ranking educational institutions in the state of Rajasthan, and among the Muslim minority community in India. Financial help has come from various sources including Islamic Development Bank of Saudi Arabia.

Tremendous progress has been made by the society in the field of Muslim minority education, particularly women's education, through sustained struggle, dedicated efforts, generous help, moral support and encouragement.

Anjuman's efforts are worth emulating; and they show what managements can really do in the field of Muslim minority education through constructive approach and leadership. Spoon-feeding cannot be a substitute for sustained and sincere efforts; and this is the path of progress for any backward minority community in the field of education.

From *Muflis* and *Lawaris* schools, the Anjuman turned them into economically viable and self-reliant institutions in the service of the larger community, especially, the Muslims. The Anjuman truly stands for the 'Cause of Education'.

Madina Educational Society (Hyderabad)

Madina Educational Society in Hyderabad has made big strides in the field of education. They have 60 years of history and 10 years of record of service in the field of education. They are running about eight institutions, such as, public schools, junior colleges for boys and girls, including Madina Education Centre.

Their objectives are to:

(i) Bring renaissance in the Muslim community;
(ii) Set exemplary trend in the field of education; and
(iii) Strive for communal harmony.

Madina Education Centre is a modern centre of education. Its aims are:

(i) To train students to think in the right perspective
(ii) To eradicate undue orthodoxy
(iii) To develop clearcut positive concepts of religious, cultural, social norms and values
(iv) To work for Hindu-Muslim unity and promotion of national integration

(v) To study and prepare comprehensive programmes for the educational upliftment of the Muslim minority

(vi) To determine Muslim's positive role in the wider national perspective

(vii) To rediscover Islamic intellectual and academic achievements and their presentation to modern media

(viii) To synchronize with contemporary intellectual awakening and scientific thinking

(ix) To discourage extravagant wastages in marriages and other rituals

The society has a dynamic secretary who is the driving force behind all activities of the society.

In contrast, there are also some groups of people among the minorities who have set up schools and colleges to exploit the Muslim minority in the name of their welfare.

The Muslim minority community needs much more of such dynamic and dedicated leadership; and organizations to help the cause of educational development of the Muslim minority community which alone can remove their educational, social and economic backwardness and poverty.

Christian Organization

The Church of North India (CNI) (Nagpur)

The Church of North India is a united church which evolved out of a union of the following six churches on 29 November, 1970, at Nagpur, Maharashtra.

(i) The Council of Baptist Churches in Northern India

(ii) The Church of the Brethren in India

(iii) The Disciples of Christ

(iv) The Church of India

(v) The Methodist Church

(vi) The United Church of Northern India

The badge of the CNI represents a symbol of eternity.

Area

All the states of the Indian union except for the four states of South India, are within the bounds of the Church of North India. It covers 80% of the area and 75% of the population in India. Nine regional languages, as well as Hindi and English, and six major tribal languages are used within the CNI area. All the cultural differences of Indian people are to be found within this Church with its congregations dispersed throughout the villages, towns and cities of a vast territory.

The poor and social justice for them are the major concern of CNI.

Education

In the area of education, The CNI has made great strides. It runs the following types of educational institutions:

Degree Colleges	12
Inter Colleges	30
Secondary Schools	150
Primary Schools	500
Technical Institutions	03
Agricultural Institutes	02

The services rendered by the CNI in the field of education among not only Christians of all denominations but all other communities are noteworthy in terms of quantity as well as quality.

Parsi Organization and Institution

The Bai Avabi Framji Petit Parsi Girls' Orphanage (Mumbai)

Several trusts of the Parsis under the name of 'Petit' are given to the promotion of education facilities, particularly for the poor and the needy.

They are running three schools which bear the name 'petit'. These schools cater for courses leading to the S.S.C. and I.C.S.C. examinations.

The school teaching for the I.C.S.C. is governed by the Central Board of Education whose rules and regulations permit the school to function as a minority community managed institution having full control of its administrative and financial management.

But in the schools teaching for S.S.C. under the Government of Maharashtra, the minority managed institutes are debarred from exercising administrative and financial controls.

The Government of Maharashtra enacted three Acts:

(i) The Secondary School Code which is applicable to all schools.

(ii) The Maharashtra Employees of Private School — Conditions of Service Rules 1981.

(iii) The Maharashtra Educational Institutions Management Act which provides for the taking over the management of property owned by educational institutions.

Encroachment on Right given by the Organization

Schedule A 1(a) of the Maharashtra Employees of Private School — Conditions of Service Rules 1981, stipulates the constitution of a school committee which would be responsible to the Government of Maharashtra for the management of the school; this is at variance with the trust deed of a minority community managed institutions.

Rule 3 of the said Schedule A relating to management and regulation of the finance of the school, appointment, etc., according to them, is *ultra vires* to the Constitution as it violates the rights guaranteed to a minority community.

Legal Opinion

Their legal advisors M/s Crawford Bayley and Co. gave the opinion that they were not governed by the Bombay Primary Education Act 1947, and the Bombay Municipal Corporation Act 1988.

Yet, the Education Department of the Bombay Municipal Corporation compelled them to seek recognition and demand compliance with various orders and directives concerning financial and administrative matters which they consider, are entirely the responsibilities of the trustees and the management of the trust.

Result

They never expressed any objection in complying with requests for statistical data, etc. They thought that such recognition would entitle the school to:

(i) present their pupils at all public examinations;

(ii) present pupils as candidates for scholarship examination; and

(iii) apply for registration for grants-in-aid from the education fund.

A possible implication of the provisions of the Bombay Municipal Corporation Act imposes an obligation on the corporation to provide for the maintenance of primary schools.

Parsi institutions except for schools under the name of 'Petit' are well established, having almost no grievance.

However, some of the grievances, may be very minor or small, the Parsi managed educational institutions, require utmost attention of the concerned authorities. The institutions bearing the name 'Petit' deserve particular attention from the concerned authorities as well as the community.

TEN

Non-financial and other Grievances of the Minority Managed Educational Institutions Aggregated

An overview of non-financial and other grievances of the minority managed educational institutions statewise is presented in this chapter; some grievances are common and universal and some are specific to a particular state situation.

Andhra Pradesh

(i) The delay in recognition was common. The reason assigned was corruption in education department.

The government laid down several conditions including appointment of staff. Thus official recognition got unnecessarily delayed by the authorities, due to the indifferent attitude of the concerned authority. The permission to open new classes and recognition of these classes were not given.

(ii) Complicated procedures and lot of unnecessary and avoidable paperwork created difficulty.

(iii) There is grievance on account of permission not being given to start technical education institutions.

Neither All India Technical Education Council (AITEC) nor Osmania University nor the State Government gave permission to start technical education institutions by the minorities. Ten proposals has been rejected so far.

(iv) Redtapism in education department created a lot of problems.

(v) Getting recognition and renewal of recognition every year entail a lot of paperworks and files to pile up; as a result, lot of time, money and efforts were wasted by the management.

About fifty applications filed by Classic Education Society, Hyderabad about recognition remained uncomplied.

(vi) Untrained teachers, especially in some subjects, and unfilled vacancies of teaching positions for want of good candidates, were also baneful to the quality of education.

(vii) There were very few competent teachers.

(viii) General conditions were not so good.

(ix) There was lack of element of competitiveness, particularly, among educational institutions of Muslim minority.

(x) Some groups or individuals take undue advantage of the Constitutional provisions. They set up schools and colleges and use them to their own purpose, as a means of exploitation, as alleged by some respondents.

Bihar

(i) There are a plethora of rules of the Bihar Government. The rules are interpreted by the government functionaries to the disadvantage of the minorities. This is a subject of detailed study, according to some respondents.

(ii) There are grievances against the behaviour of the government functionaries. They do not behave well. They are arrogant.

(iii) Lot of certificates and documents have to be submitted for the proof of minority status.

(iv) Unnecessary interference by the educational authorities on the pretext of maintaining educational standards was alleged.

(v) Affiliation fee is very high.

(vi) Facilities in schools depended upon the collection from students. Community assistance did not come forth.

(vii) Teaching aid, classroom facilities, indoor games, sports facilities were very much inadequate.

(viii) The posts of teachers were very often not sanctioned.

(ix) The appointment of teachers did not take place through advertisement and interview.

(x) The Pardah Nasheen Girls Schools have more grievances both financial and non-financial. They did not have regular grants, much inadequate staff, almost no teaching aid, no good facilities of classrooms, toilets, etc., poor community support. Girls' education was very much neglected.

Chandigarh

(i) Most of the institutions do not have properly constituted Governing Body.

(ii) The teachers' representation in the Governing Body was inadequate.

(iii) The management was simply not concerned about the problem of the institution.

(iv) The government authorities were totally neglectful.

(v) Some teachers had to go to the Supreme Court on account of termination of their services.

(vi) No initiative came from the government to strengthen the existing facilities and faculties.

Delhi

(i) Delay in recognition was alleged.

(ii) Interference in admission policy was also alleged.

(iii) Educational aids, films, books ought to be provided to these institutions.

(iv) Teaching aid was inadequate.

(v) There were lack of qualified teachers to teach in Urdu medium.

(vi) There were generally lack of competent and qualified teachers. The recruitment was reported to be not on merit generally.

(vii) Seats should be reserved for linguistic and religious minorities in teachers' Training institutions, the teachers felt.

(viii) In some institutions the laboratory assistant was not cooperative, said the students.

(ix) Students of minority institutions get conditioned by biased teaching.

(x) Harassment of clean shaven Sikh students was alleged in Sikh institutions.

(xi) Lack of parents' cooperation was alleged.

(xii) Dearth of books, as according to syllabus; in Urdu language particularly, was alleged.

(xiii) In some institutions librarian's post was lying vacant for more than five years.

(xiv) Laboratory facilities were almost non-existent and practicals were not done.

(xv) The problem of space is very crucial, land cost in Delhi is very high, no aid is given for purchase of land.

(xvi) Prosperous group of people among Muslims send their children to good schools. Only the children from less prosperous groups or weaker sections come to minority schools. They are not interested because no job is available.

Karnataka

(i) Parents did not cooperate.

(ii) Students were least interested in study.

(iii) Government should do their utmost to improve the standard of education among the minorities.

(iv) Permission to open a school should be given only to those who had knowledge and experience in the field of school education.

(v) Surprise visit by Education Officers was necessary.

(vi) Refresher training from time to time ought to be arranged.

(vii) Teachers were subjected to harassment by the head of the institutions in some cases.

(viii) The pay commission's recommendations were not fully implemented.

(ix) Recognition was delayed for the last four years for a school run by Blue Nile Education Society, Mysore.

(x) The attitude of the government officials was not unbiased, as was alleged in some cases.

(xi) Chances of promotion were nil.

(xii) In some cases, sometimes, employment was on contract basis, and the post was not being made permanent (for teachers).

(xiii) The government nearly forced Al-Ameen College in Bangalore to close its language course in Urdu, and asked the college to send their students to government institutions.

Kerala

(i) The behaviour of management against teaching staff was suppressive and feudal type.

(ii) Even the unaided schools were harassed by bureaucrats from education department.

(iii) Procedural delays consumed a greater part of the time and energy.

(iv) The management did not provide free and fair atmosphere for the teaching staff.
(v) The sanction of post was always delayed.
(vi) Government rules were impractical and generally caused hardship to the school management.
(vii) U.M.H. High School Malappuram did not have even basic facilities, no electricity, no space for staff room, no drinking water, no separate toilet for women staff.
(viii) Syllabus should be broadened; in such a way as to give freedom to schools to teach religion, morality and ethics to students.
(ix) Commuting facilities were very poor for students.
(x) Matters relating to the recognition of schools and affiliation of colleges were not taken up favourably.
(xi) Students were organized by the political parties. This spoilt the academic atmosphere, said the principal of a college.
(xii) Work was disrupted when the outsiders interfered on the pretext of "educational standard".

Maharashtra

(i) There was dispute in management in Urdu High School, Buldana, owing to the report by the Charity Commissioner.
(ii) Budget was not prepared for so many years.
(iii) The term fee grants of the school were not utilized properly.
(iv) The headmaster of the school who belonged to one group did not cooperate with the managing committee of the rival group.
(v) Students were automatically promoted resulting into their weak foundation.
(vi) Trained teachers for Arabic were not available.
(vii) Ulamah Fazlahs should be declared eligible for entry into training, such as, B.Ed., M.Ed., Courses by all universities.
(viii) There should be provision of refresher course for teachers.
(ix) Textbooks and other relevant materials should be suppliea in time.
(x) Government should give loan without interest for construction work of the school.
(xi) The sanction of teachers' posts on the basis of recognized

number of sections resulted in partial allocation of funds and teaching positions which in turn inhibits the development of the school.

(xii) Interference by the District Education authorities were unnecessary and avoidable at least in unaided autonomous schools.

(xiii) Special grants should be given to primary education, technical education, vocational education, and girls education.

(xiv) Government should provide land, electricity and water; free of cost to minority institutions.

Mizoram

(i) Teaching facilities were not adequate.

(ii) Development of the institutions are hindered due to lack of resources.

(iii) Politicians interfere in the selection of teaching and non-teaching staff, as a result, selection is generally not based on merit.

(iv) There was usually delay in sanctioning the post.

Orissa

(i) The teaching staff was inadequate.

(ii) The facilities enjoyed by the teachers of the government schools were not available to the teachers of the minority schools.

(iii) Audio-visual aid, furniture, etc., were inadequate.

Punjab

(i) The role of school/college management was not positive; it should be marginalized.

(ii) Rules regarding leave were not followed, and the staff suffered a great deal.

(iii) Selection of teachers was not usually on the basis of merit.

(iv) Teaching aids, facilities of hostel, libraries, recreation centre, sports, facilities for day scholars were inadequate.

(v) Low parental guidance and motivation.

(vi) Management's indifference.

(vii) Students' indifference towards studies.

(viii) No housing facility.
(ix) No training facility.
(x) Not much promotional avenue.
(xi) No incentive for good work.

Tamil Nadu

(i) Long leave of different categories was not sanctioned immediately.
(ii) Leave vacancies, short-term vacancies were not filled up due to inordinate delay in sanctioning post by government.
(iii) Parents do not pay much attention to the attendance and studies of the students.
(iv) There was procedural delay in sanctioning additional posts/ filling existing vacancies due to retirement and maternity leave.
(v) There was delay in approving of the appointment made in permanent post.
(vi) There was delay in approving of the promotion made.
(vii) There was delay in getting approval for making fresh appointments.
(viii) The post was not sanctioned in which a teacher was working for ten years in a school.
(ix) There was inordinate delay in sanctioning the post; therefore, the salary was withheld for a year.
(x) Some Muslim institutions' managements have implicitly adopted a policy of selecting teachers from only non-Muslim communities.
(xi) The additional post of professor is never created; as a result, the teachers feel dejected.
(xii) The management is pursuing neither a policy of merit nor a policy of favour to the Minority Community. The post is filled up by the highest bidder among the qualified.
(xiii) The head of the institution instead of acting as educational administrator is usually bent upon fulfilling the whims and fancies of the management.
(xiv) There is no training for non-teaching staff which results in inefficiency.
(xv) Even after more than a decade, the recognition is not granted.

(xvi) Adequate staff was not provided, and no non-teaching post was allotted in primary school.

(xvii) For every three years lot of certificates are required to be produced for getting temporary recognition.

(xviii) Academic load was heavy.

(xix) Teachers and head of the institution are treated like slaves by the management.

(xx) It is difficult to get trained teachers for Urdu medium.

Uttar Pradesh

(i) Official recognition takes so much of time in communication.

(ii) In scores of cases, recognition was delayed for more than a decade.

(iii) Private institutions are forced to give bribes to get recognition.

(iv) The government ordered to admit more students but did not allow to open new sections nor did it sanction any additional post.

(v) There was too much government interference.

(vi) The sanctioned posts of teachers were quite insufficient to the strength of students in schools.

(vii) Every type of hindrance was existing for recognition, registration of professional, technical and training institutions.

(viii) Minority institution's status was always delayed and given only after much harassment.

(ix) The procedure to get approval of the appointment is cumbersome.

(x) Appointment of teachers for new sections was always delayed.

(xi) Maladministration and lack of effective management had been alleged.

(xii) Attitude of the head of the institution was not encouraging and cooperative.

West Bengal

(i) Drinking water facilities in several educational institutions, particularly in Darjeeling region, were very much inadequate.

Summary

If we sum up, the following common non-financial and other miscellaneous grievances come to the fore:

(i) There was generally a gap between the establishment and the recognition of a minority educational institution of unreasonable duration. In many cases, the gap was too long. In many other cases, the recognition had been pending for more than ten years. So, the delay in according recognition was a common grievance.

There are several conditions laid down, complicated procedures, unnecessary and avoidable paperwork, indifferent attitude of the concerned authority, corrupt practices in the concerned department, non-compliance of application and letters, etc., delay the accord of recognition. The difficulty in recognition was a common grievance.

(ii) In some of the states, there is grievance on account of denial of permission to start institution of technical education.

(iii) Renewal of recognition every year which again requires a lot of paperwork and files to pile up, also wastage of money and time, was another area of grievance.

(iv) A plethora of rules, interpreted by the government functionaries to the disadvantage of the minority institutions in terms of determining and declaring their minority status creates difficulties.

(v) Lot of certificates and documents to be submitted for the proof of minority status overburden the office with paperwork.

(vi) Indifference and arrogant behaviour of the government functionaries.

(vii) Unnecessary interference by the educational authorities on the pretext of maintaining 'educational standards' and 'excellence'.

(viii) Not so qualified and untrained teachers especially in some subjects, like Urdu, Arabic, etc.

(ix) Dearth of books, as according to syllabus, in language medium, particularly Urdu medium.

(x) Inadequate or sometimes non-existent teaching aids, audio-visual aids, classroom facilities, facilities of games and sports, drinking water, separate toilet facilities for boys and girls, etc.

(xi) Vacant posts of teachers and library staff, unsanctioned posts, difficulty in obtaining sanction of posts, and approval of appointments and promotions made to teaching posts.

(xii) Poor living and service conditions of the teaching and non-teaching staff.

(xiii) Non-availability of grievance redressal machinery, difficulty of teachers in the event of termination of their services.

(xiv) Court cases between rival groups in the Government Bodies, between the teaching and non-teaching staff on the one hand and management on the other.

(xv) Lack of concern on the part of management for the educational institution.

(xvi) Feudal outlook and attitude of the members of management.

(xvii) Interference of the politicians and party groups in the affairs of the institution particularly among the students.

(xviii) Lack of willingness and concern on the part of the local community, local leaders, etc.

(xix) Apathy of the parents due to various reasons, such as, illiteracy, poverty, backwardness, etc.

(xx) Automatic promotion of students from one class to another at the primary, middle and secondary levels.

(xxi) Drop-outs among the children, particularly, at the primary and middle levels.

(xxii) Dearth of competent, qualified, and dedicated teachers.

(xxiii) Narrow groupism among teaching and non-teaching staff.

(xxiv) At times, partisan attitude of the head of the institution, or, members of the Governing Body.

(xxv) Delay in sanctioning leave of different types; leave rules not being followed.

(xxvi) Heavy academic burden on teachers, and load on students.

(xxvii) Difficulty in registration and recognition of professional, technical and training institutions.

(xxviii) Indifference towards girls' education, particularly among the Muslims and the Buddhists.

This is not the case with the Christians, the Sikhs, and the Parsis. In these communities sometimes, the girls outnumber the boys in the field of education.

The major areas of grievances related to:

(a) Recognition of the institution.

(b) Recruitment of teachers.

(c) Service conditions of teaching and non-teaching staff.

(d) Training of teaching staff, particularly, Urdu and Arabic teachers.

(e) Medium of instruction, particularly, books, reading materials, etc., in Urdu.

The real concern should not be only to propagate education but also to provide quality education of general, technical, professional and vocational type.

ELEVEN

Conclusion: Outcome and Recommendations

The scenario of education among the minority managed educational institutions in India is not the same in all regions; nor was it very sanguine. It presented a mixed kind of picture of the situation. It varied from state to state; region to region; institution to institution and management to management. It was struck by lack of coherence and uniformity.

However, the minority educational institutions and their managements faced some common problems, and had some common grievances.

Some major non-financial grievances of the minority managed educational institutions related to:

(i) recognition
(ii) affiliation
(iii) medium of teaching
(iv) recruitment and training of teaching staff
(v) admission
(vi) curriculum, teaching aids, etc.
(vii) attitude of parents and students
(viii) regulatory measures and disciplinary control
(ix) constitution of the management committee
(x) determination of the minority status, etc.

The Buddhist and the Muslim minorities were educationally more backward, and much less competitive. The Christians, the Parsis and the Sikhs were educationally more progressive and relatively much more competitive. Yet, there were some common grievances of all the minorities educational institutions. Their grievances were (i) financial, (ii) managerial, and (iii) situational.

In view of these several common grievances, outcome of suggestions and recommendations on the basis of our analysis and study is presented here.

Good Administration for the Sake of Good Education: Reasonable Regulation

The right of minority managed educational institutions to appoint principal, headmaster and other staff; their right to terminate the services of the staff after proper enquiry should not be restricted or interfered with.

But at the same time, it must be borne in mind that the right to administration of educational institutions did not mean the right to maladministration. The state might prescribe reasonable regulations to ensure the excellence of the minority institutions.

This, in fact, must ensure two things:

(i) The management should well administer the institution; and

(ii) The government functionaries in Education Department must act fairly and impartially without prejudice, and must not unnecessarily interfere in the name of 'prescribing regulations to ensure the excellence of the minority institutions'.

Basically, the aim of both the management and the government was to create conditions for good administration for the sake of good education.

All the same, for claiming the right under Article 30 of the Constitution, to administer their own educational institutions, the verdict of various courts that the institution must be an educational institution of the minorities in 'truth and reality', and not merely 'masked phantoms', must also be kept in mind.

Representation of Teachers in the Governing Body

In order to create a sense of belongingness to, and participation in the educational institution, the representation of the teaching staff on the governing body of a minority managed educational institution should not remain a debatable point. Proper representation of teaching staff on the governing body of these institutions should be given. In an age when participative management was going to be practised as a current concept, the denial of representation to the teaching staff on the governing body appeared to be beside the point. There should be proper representation of the teaching staff on the Governing Body of the minority managed institutions.

Affiliation with Reasonable Condition

A minority managed educational institution might be affiliated to a university or Board with reasonable conditions, as relating to a certain course of study in the interest of maintaining educational excellence. The conditions should not be such as to deny progress and autonomy of the institution, or, to take away the freedom of the management of administration.

Recognition should not be Rejected without Timely Communication of Reasonable Grounds

Recognition of an educational institution could be refused on a reasonable ground, e.g., needs of the community.

Recognition should not be refused on the mere ground that the school did not own a building of its own, where a building was available on lease or licence of the Trust, which proposed to start the school.

Recognition was an area where the grievance accumulated. In several cases, in some states, the recognition had been pending for more than 10 years, or, a number of applications for recognition had no compliance.

Regulatory Provisions

At times, some confusion was created on account of the interpretation of some regulatory provisions in the Constitution. By virtue of Article 30(1) two rights were guaranteed to religious minorities, viz., 'right to establish' and 'right to administer educational institutions of their own choice'.

It must be clearly understood that the extent of this right was to be determined not with reference to 'any concept of necessity or general social interest', but with 'reference to the educational institutions themselves', that is, with reference to the goal of making the institutions 'effective vehicles of education for the minority community, or other persons who resort to them.'

Any regulatory measures designed to achieve this objective should not be considered as encroachment upon the right guaranteed by Article 30(1) of the Constitution.

To illustrate: Section 19 of the Delhi Education Act, 1973 required that the scales of pay and allowances, medical facilities, pension, gratuity, provident fund and other prescribed benefits of the employees of a recognized private school should not be less than those of the employees of the corresponding status in school run by the appropriate authority.

Any procedure or regulation for enforcement of the above requirement which was aimed at attracting competent staff and thereby at the excellence of the educational institution, might be accepted as a permissible regulation, and good for the educational institution. Such regulatory measures should not be treated as an encroachment upon the right of minority.

Teaching of Urdu

Promoting the teaching of Urdu by the formation of a cooperative society of writers for publishing their works in Urdu; retention of Urdu script; adoption of a common scientific and technical terminology, were some of the recommendations of Gujral Urdu Committee (1972); these recommendations should be adopted and vigorously pursued in order to make the teaching of Urdu, or teaching of other subjects through Urdu medium truly effective.

Language Formula

Some of the minority associations, and some government agencies claimed that the language formula adopted in different states caused much strain on the minorities. For instance, in Andhra Pradesh, the state government followed 3-language formula, because of which, the minorities, whose mother tongue was other than Telugu, were forced to learn four languages. However, since learning of all these languages was relevant in one context or another, it remained to be analysed by language experts whether such strain inhibited the growth of the children or it ensured the proper development of the child and made him conversant in many languages.

Need of Balwadis and Anganwadis

It was also suggested by Andhra Pradesh Minorities Commission that primary education could be undertaken by the government through Balwadis and Anganwadis in minorities concentration areas. In a country where the poor and backward Muslim community did not send their children to schools even after the child attained six years of age, Balwadis and Anganwadis were best suited to their needs. However, the early nursing and educational care centres of the child for the weaker among the minority groups might be set up with adequate publicity and community support.

Norm for Granting Minority Status

The decision of the Basic Shiksha Parishad, Uttar Pradesh, not to grant minority status to any junior high school was unique in approach. In granting minority status, the norms evolved by the Government of India should be followed, or the states should evolve their own norms as modelled on the norms of Government of India.

Inclusion of Government Representative in Recruitment Committee

The inclusion of government representative in the Recruitment Committee was tantamount to force minorities to forfeit their right to 'administer' the institution they established. There should be no inclusion of government representative or university representative in their Recruitment Committee.

No Application of Rules of Reservation

The application of the rules of reservation in admission to the minority institution operated against the interest of the minorities. They should not be applied, or they should be applied after examining the pros and cons.

Streamlining and Modernizing the Curriculum

In relation to government schools and other non-minority schools, the curriculum which was followed in minority managed educational institutions, particularly, the Muslim Madrasa, and Buddhist monastery, was oriented to a culture of isolation of the community. Their curriculum needed to be streamlined and modernized in order to enable students to compete with the larger groups in the society.

Trained Teachers in Urdu

The posts of Urdu teachers lie vacant for years together as trained teachers in the subject were not available. Provision should be made for Ulemah, Urdu teacher/Arabic teacher to get entry into the training courses, or, orientation courses.

Review Committee

A Review Committee to look into various aspects of minorities' education at every level with due representation from minority community's eminent persons, should also be thought of.

Media Support for Awareness and Community Consciousness

Non-cooperative and uninspiring attitude of the management, teachers and students, apathy and indifference of parents were other areas of handicap in case of the minorities' educational institutions. An awareness and community consciousness was required to be created with media support, particularly, television. This might lead to greater community participation and support in terms of improved condition of funding as well as education.

To bring a Muslim minority educational institution on a par with other institutions in terms of quality of education, special attention of the government was needed. Regular and timely payment of salary to the staff; better working and living conditions for them; well equipped library and laboratory; training and orientation courses for teachers; hostel facilities to students; updated and modernized curriculum; special arrangement for the teaching of Home Science for girls; fairly good number of scholarships to students, were required to be ensured. An element of competitiveness was required to be created among these institutions.

Simplification of Rules and Procedure

In matters of recognition, rules and procedures should be simplified, grounds of rejection should be quickly communicated;

time limit in this regard should be fixed. Corruption in the system and redtapism had distorted the image of the government. This needed rectification.

Orientation Course

Regular orientation training or refresher course for teacher would be advisable in order to improve the quality of education.

Supervision and Control

Within the framework of the constitutional provisions, rules and regulations, exercising control and supervision would be advisable. The government should pay immediate attention to the minority educational institutions. Many of our respondents also felt that the Minorities Commission should send their officers to supervise all financial aid, and other educational matters from time to time. It would have a salubrious effect on the effective management and quality of education of these institutions.

Minorities Institutions must Shun Isolationism

Sir Syed Group of schools in Calcutta (who were self-supporting and were not receiving any grants) felt that the minority managed educational institutions did have a responsibility to propagate the culture of particular minority community. At the same time, they suggested that these schools should shun isolation, and be open to new ideas and common heritage of our nation.

Minorities Cell

They suggested that a provision might be made to create a Minorities Cell attached to the Directorate of Education in each state so that they could help scrutinize each proposal for grants-in-aid, accord of recognition, etc., on merit.

Simultaneously, there was another question that came into mind, whether a Directorate or Minority Cell could remove the financial and non-financial grievances of the minority managed educational institutions, if the functionaries in these organizations did not efficiently and effectively work, if the function became routinized, if the minority institutions themselves did not make efforts to grow and develop.

Preservation of Culture and Heritage: Paradox of the Parsi Institution

The Lepches changed from the Lepcha speakers to the Nepali speakers under the influence of the Nepalese in the Himalayan region of Darjeeling and Sikkim. The young Parsis changed from Parsi Gujarati to English speakers. They had turned 'Parsenglish'. So there was a decline in the Parsi culture. Parsis changed from Parsi Gujarati speakers to Parsi-English. It was open to question how far the education institutions of this minority group (Parsis) had been able to preserve their culture and heritage — which was what the Indian Constitution, by granting the 'right to establish and administer educational institutions' meant to achieve. The Supreme Court Judgment on St. Stephen's College Delhi, and Allahabad Agriculture College, regarding minorities' rights to establish and administer educational institutions related to preservation of their culture, tradition and heritage.

In the changing context of society, over the past century and during the last few decades of the present century, the Parsi Minority Community had been greatly transformed, particularly, in respect of their culture and tradition. They had became more, 'anglicized' or 'westernized'. This was reflected from their own educational institutions which the Parsis had been running.

The Government of Maharashtra did not discriminate between institutions in the name of religion. At the same time, the religious minorities, as it was envisaged in the Indian Constitution, would establish their own institution and administer them. The Parsis had their own Trusts, Councils, Charities and Panchayats which were instrumental behind their educational institutions. Yet Parsi community was on decline. Preservation of their culture was in crisis.

Side by side, there were certain other factors to be taken into account. The increasing pace of urbanization particularly in metropolitan city like Mumbai, the city of Surat in Gujarat, which remained the seat of Parsis; their openness to wider external influences, particularly the modern West; their entry into professions, business, and industry (for some decades of this century, the Parsis remained as top class business and industrial section (Tatas, Godrej, etc.); these influences when combined together, created a revolutionary change in the world outlook of the Parsis, particularly, the youth. The equality of sexes was more sharply visible among them. They had also formed an Intermarriage Parsi Gujarati Association under the changed situation, which was further in the process of change. In their case, one cannot see any harmony between the spirit of the Constitution and the spirit and aspirations of the people. The people were much ahead of their time and the spirit of the Constitution (to establish and administer institutions for preservation of culture and heritage). All the Parsi institutions had become anglicized and westernized. This was the crisis of the present situation, and the crisis became more aggravating when the community was small and urbane.

Need of the Buddhist Educational Institution

The Buddhist educational institutions were very much scattered; it was no easy task to get the precise information about them.

(i) There was no dispute regarding the Constitution of the Buddhist Managing Committee. Their Managing Committee was elected.
The Buddhist institution had its own Committee to look after the maintenance of the institution.

(ii) The institution had its own method of teaching.

(iii) Only male students were allowed in the monastery. They gave education in Tibetology to the Lamas from the primary stage. They had no provision for education of female.

Very much like the education in the Muslim Madrasa, the education in the Buddhist monastery needed to be modernized in order to cater to the changing needs of the monastery as well as the mainstream of the social life of the Buddhist.

A Comprehensive and Uniform Policy Required

(i) A comprehensive and uniform policy keeping in view the problems and conditions of the minorities institutions might be evolved and adopted, and regulations be framed in regard to,

(a) recognition

(b) recruitment of teachers

(c) admission of students, particularly in vocational, technical and professional institutions, at the national level by the Minorities Commission. In this respect, the norms evolved by the Minorities Commission in December 1998 and the Department of Education, Government of India in October 1989, regarding recognition and recruitment of teachers, should be unequivocally accepted by the states and implemented.

(ii) Similarly at the state level, within the broad framework of the above policy and regulations, norms might be laid down for

(a) recognition;

(b) recruitment;

(c) admission of students in vocational, technical and professional institutions.

(iii) The administrative delay in these matters which had become the order of the day, was indefensible. It could be avoided if reasons were assigned for not giving recognition as stipulated in the norms and principles evolved by the Minorities Commission, and also the Government of India.

Norms might be laid down and followed in admission for students of the particular minority community, and also for students of other community within the framework of the judicial pronouncements of the Supreme Court of India (in St. Stephen's College, Delhi; and Agriculture College, Allahabad case). However, the situation would differ from region to region, institution to institution, and one minority group to another minority group. This would call for some flexibility and imaginative application of the judicial pronouncements.

The National Policy on Education and the Programme of Action which were formulated by the Department of Education, Ministry of Human Resource Development, Government of India, envisaged that guidelines for recognition of the minority managed educational institutions and for the timely disposal of applications for such a recognition should be laid down. Accordingly, each State Government/Union Territory was expected to formulate its recognition policy and give wider publicity to the same.

The Minorities Commission also prepared a set of guidelines for determination of minority status, recognition and related matters in respect of minority educational institutions, and circulated the same to the State Government/Union Territories in December, 1988, for facilitating the formulation of these guidelines by them, since much progress could not be made by many States and Union Territories administrations in evolving these guidelines and norms, the Department of Education, Government of India evolved broad policy norms and principles for recognition of minority managed educational institutions other than those meant exclusively for imparting religious instruction, and forwarded them in October 1989 to the State Government/Union Territories for appropriate action at their end.

These policy norms and principles are given as hereunder:

Minorities Commission, Government of India. Guidelines for Determination of Minority Status. Recognition and related matters in respect of minority educational institutions under the Constitution of India.

1. Determination of Minority Character of an Educational Institution

The benefits of Article 30(1) can be claimed by the community only on proving that it is a religious or linguistic minority and the institution was established by it. The question of proof in a Court of Law is regulated by the provision of the Indian Evidence Act. This Act requires that when there is a written document, other evidence is to be excluded but if there is no written document, other evidence is admissible.

2. Objects of Establishment of Minority Educational Institution

It is not always necessary that the objects for which a minority may establish an educational institution must include the conservation of its language, script, or culture. Article 30(1) only emphasizes that the body establishing and administering an educational institution belongs to a minority based on religion or language. It says nothing about the character of education to be imparted by them. Hence, an institution will be a minority institution, even if it imparts secular education. Once it is proved to be a minority institution, the character of education to be imparted and of administration will be at the choice of those who can administer it. In these matters, the choice cannot be of any one else.

3. Fulfilment of Statutory Requirements for Seeking Recognition

An institution seeking recognition must fulfil the statutory requirements concerning the academic standards, the qualifications of teachers, and of the students seeking admission. It must have the financial resources and the capability to run on a sustained basis. When the applications seeking recognition are not considered favourably, grounds of rejection must be communicated to the educational institutions filling such applications so as to enable them to overcome obstacles to their early recognition.

4. Medium of Instruction in Minority Educational Institutions

The State Government or the university is not empowered to prescribe the medium of instruction to be followed by minority educational institutions. However, in case of institutions receiving grants-in-aid, there are certain standards of proficiency to be observed. No decision, within our knowledge lays down that teaching of a State language compulsorily is within such conditions for grant-of-aid. But, if such a condition is laid down, the institution receiving the aid will be well advised to observe it.

5. Constitution of Governing Bodies in Minority Educational Institutions

The minority educational institutions must be free to induct competent and reputed individuals from other communities in the Managing Committees/Governing Bodies. The minority character of an institution is not impaired so long as the constitution of the Managing Committee/Governing Body provides for an effective majority to the members of the minority community.

The State should not have any power, directly or through the university, to direct the constitution of the governing bodies in a manner so as to deprive a minority of the effective administration of its educational institutions. However, the State or the university may lay down general guidelines to ensure that only qualified persons find a place in the Governing Bodies.

6. Disciplinary Control over Staff in Minority Educational Institutions

While the management should exercise the disciplinary control over staff, it must be ensured that the management hold an inquiry and follow a fair procedure before punishment is given. With a view to preventing the possible misuse of power by the management of the minority educational institutions, the State has the regulatory power to safeguard the interests of their employees and their service conditions including procedure for punishments to be imposed.

7. Admission of Students in Minority Educational Institutions

The minority educational institutions must have the freedom to give special consideration to the students of their own community in matters of admission. The government should not insist on admission in these institutions being thrown open to all, strictly in order of merit. The government cannot enforce the rules of reservation in favour of Scheduled Castes, Scheduled Tribes, and other backward communities for admission of students in these institutions.

In granting admissions to children belonging to the minority community itself, rules of natural justice and fair play must be applied and donations or other extraneous factors should not be allowed so as to discriminate against the less advantaged children from the same minority community.

8. Appointment of Teachers in Minority Educational Institutions

The government cannot enforce the rules of reservation in favour of Scheduled Castes, Scheduled Tribes and other backward classes for the posts of teachers and other staff in minority educational institutions.

Government of India, Ministry of Human Resources Development and Department of Education: Policy Norms and Principles for Recognition of Minority Managed Educational Institutions other than those meant Exclusively for Imparting Religious Instruction

1. Minorities can be based either on religion or on language.

2. Minorities may be in terms of a religious or linguistic community which is numerically less than 50 per cent of the population of the State concerned.
3. The agency managing the educational institution will have to possess some legal status — an Association of persons registered under the Societies Registration Act or a body with corporate soul, etc.
4. Admission into minority managed educational institutions need not be confined to members of the minority.
5. Right to administer educational institutions shall be subject to reasonable regulations, which may include:
   (a) stipulations regarding conditions of recognition by relevant authorities (such as Directorate of Education, Boards of Secondary Education, Universities, AICTE);
   (b) qualifications and conditions of service of teachers;
   (c) a requirement that the educational institutions run by a minority shall do nothing which may come in the way of communal and social harmony;
   (d) a requirement that the institution will not use its privilege as minority administered institution for pecuniary benefit of an individual or group;
   (e) disciplinary rules of the institutions in respect of their teaching and non-teaching staff being consistent with principles of natural justices;
   (f) observance of principles of sound administration;
   (g) enforcement of general laws of the land pertaining to the educational institutions concerned.
6. The minority managed educational institutions shall have the freedom to appoint any qualified candidate, but it would be advisable for them to select teachers and other employees through employment exchange or open advertisement.
7. Teachers in minority managed educational institutions should possess requisite qualifications.
8. The regulations shall not be such as to render the constitutional rights of the minorities nugatory for example:

(a) conditions that the government shall have the right to take over the management of the institution;
(b) that the government shall have powers to constitute managing committees;
(c) that the Governing Body of the institution shall include persons other than members of the minority community;
(d) that the government can require the institution to reserve seats;
(e) that scholars of the institution would not be eligible to opportunities in higher education;
(f) that the government shall have the right to insist on use of any language as the medium of instruction;
(g) that the institution shall not charge fees from students, etc.

The stipulations should be regulatory and/or educational in character and conducive to making the institutions effective vehicles of education for minority communities.

9. There shall be no discrimination between minority and majority educational institutions in the matter of sanctioning grants-in-aid. Such grants-in-aid can be made conditional upon appropriate regulatory measures to ensure that the funds are used for purposes for which they are sanctioned.
10. Minority managed educational institutions receiving State aid
    (a) shall not deny admission to persons outside the minority on grounds of religion, caste, language, etc.;
    (b) shall not, without the consent of the pupil or his guardian, impart religious instruction or compel students to attend religious workshop.
11. Procedures should be clearly laid down in respect of:
    (a) eligibility of a society/trust to be treated as minority;
    (b) competent authority to grant recognition;

(c) time limits for making decision.

12. Where recognition is not considered favourably, grounds of rejection shall be communicated to the educational institution to help it overcome obstacles in the way of recognition.

Modelled on these norms and principles, the State Governments and Union Territories administrations ought to evolve their own guidelines for recognition of the minority managed educational institutions; and wide publicity should be given to them through national and regional newspapers and television programmes. The publicity could be given in English, Hindi, Urdu and various local languages of the region, so that the agency claiming to manage such institutions would be fully aware, and should have no cause of grievance in regard to the recognition of the institutions established by them.

However, item no. 12 of the policy norms and principles as circulated by the Department of Education, Government of India, should receive careful attention:

"Where recognition is not considered favourably, grounds of rejection shall be communicated to the educational institution to help it overcome obstacles in the way of recognition."

During our investigation it transpired that the communication about the grounds of rejection of recognition was generally not made, or the communication took its own time. It was here that the bureaucratic or procedural delay or even arrogance on the part of the government functionary was reported. The institution suffered a sense of discrimination and neglect by the concerned authority, or often complained of 'corruption' in the concerned department. This led to the accumulation of grievance. It must also be conceded that the matter of recognition was a major area of grievance among the minority managed educational institutions. Specific guidelines on the model of the norms prepared by the Government of India ought to be evolved by the States and Union Territories Administrations; or the guidelines prepared by the Centre ought to be accepted by the States. If the States did not prepare the guidelines within a specific period, the Minorities Commission, now with their statutory status, could prevail upon the Government of India and State Governments to accept the guidelines circulated by the Department of Education, Government of India in October 1989.

At the same time, the guidelines formulated were circulated by the Minorities Commission, Government of India, regarding

(a) determination of minority character of an educational institution,
(b) objects of establishment of minority educational institution,
(c) fulfilment of statutory requirements for seeking recognition,
(d) constitution of Governing Body,
(e) disciplinary control over staff,
(f) admission of students,
(g) appointment of teachers, in minority educational institutions, might also be used as a useful instrument by the States/Union Territories administrations for evolving their own guidelines.

As a matter of fact, the guidelines issued in December 1988 by the Minorities Commission; and norms and principles for recognition of minority managed educational institutions, circulated by the Government of India, Department of Education, in October 1989, should be together used to evolve guidelines by various States and Union Territories administrations. This process of evolving guidelines ought to be completed by various States and Union Territories administrations at the earliest to promote the interest of the education of the minorities.

Beyond the stipulated period, the Minorities Commission might use their good offices to prevail upon the States and Union Territories administrations to accept the guidelines evolved by the Government of India. A time-bound policy approach in this matter would be needed.

Appendices

APPENDIX I

A COMPARATIVE CHART OF THE LEVEL OF ACHIEVEMENT OF VARIOUS MINORITY MANAGED EDUCATIONAL INSTITUTIONS

Level of Achievement	MMEI	BMEI	CHRMEI	PARM EI	SIMEI
Level of Competitiveness	Low	Low	High	Medium	Medium
Level of Self-support	Low	Low	High	Low	Low
Level of Community Support	Low	Medium	Medium	High	High
Level of Fund Generating Capacity	Low	Low	High	Medium	Medium

MMEI - Muslim Managed Educational Institutions
BMEI - Buddhist Managed Educational Institutions
CHRMEI - Christian Managed Educational Institutions
PARMEI - Parsi Managed Educational Institutions
SIMEI - Sikh Managed Educational Institutions

APPENDIX II

A COMPARATIVE CHART OF THE LEVEL OF GRIEVANCES AMONG VARIOUS MINORITY MANAGED EDUCATIONAL INSTITUTIONS

Type and Level of Grievances	MMEI	BMEI	CHRMEI	PARMEI	SIMEI
Financial Grievances	High	Medium	Low	Low	Low
Non-Financial and other Miscellaneous Grievances	High	Medium	Medium	Low	Medium

APPENDIX III
THE TYPE OF GRIEVANCES (THE GENERAL TREND) IN MINORITY MANAGED EDUCATIONAL INSTITUTIONS

Sl. No.	*State/U.T.*	*Delay in Grants*	*Inadequate Grants*	*Delay in Release of Grants Over Long Period*	*Trouble and Cumbersome Rules for Grants*
1.	Andhra Pradesh	Yes	Yes	Yes	Yes
2.	Bihar	Yes	Yes	Yes	Yes
3.	Chandigarh	Yes	-	-	-
4.	Delhi	Yes	Yes	-	-
5.	Gujarat	Yes	-	Yes	-
6.	Karnataka	Yes	Yes	Yes	-
7.	Kerala	Yes	Yes	Yes	-
8.	Maharashtra	Yes	Yes	Yes	-
9.	Orissa	Yes	Yes	Yes	-
10.	Punjab	Yes	Yes	-	-
11.	Tamil Nadu	Yes	Yes	-	-
12.	Uttar Pradesh	Yes	Yes	Yes	Yes
13.	West Bengal	Yes	Yes	Yes	-

APPENDIX IV
MISCELLANEOUS FACTORS RELATED TO MMEI

Sl. No.	*State/U.T.*	*Lack of Parents Cooperations*	*Lack of Syllabus Books in Urdu*	*Lack of Trained Teachers in Urdu/ Arabic Language*
1.	Andhra Pradesh			
2.	Bihar			
3.	Chandigarh			
4.	Delhi	Yes	Yes	Yes
5.	Gujarat			
6.	Karnataka	Yes	-	-
7.	Kerala	Yes	-	Yes
8.	Maharashtra			
9.	Orissa			
10.	Punjab			
11.	Tamil Nadu	Yes	-	Yes

APPENDIX V
GRIEVANCES IN MMEI

Sl. No.	*Stae/U.T.*	*Maintenance Grants are not Released*	*Teachers get Less than Prescribed Scale*	*Teachers Harassed by Management Head*	*Post not made Permanent for Long Period*	*Salary Withheld for long Period*
1.	Andhra Pradesh	Yes	Yes	Yes	Yes	Yes
2.	Bihar	Yes	Yes	-	-	-
3.	Chandigarh	-	-	-	-	Yes
4.	Delhi	-	-	-	-	-
5.	Gujarat	-	Yes	Yes	Yes	-
6.	Karnataka	Yes	-	-	Yes	-
7.	Kerala	Yes	Yes	Yes	-	-
8.	Maharashtra	-	-	Yes	-	-
9.	Orissa	-	-	-	-	-
10.	Punjab	-	-	Yes	-	-
11.	Tamil Nadu	Yes	Yes	Yes	Yes	Yes

APPENDIX VI
GRIEVANCES IN MMEI

Sl. No.	*State/U.T.*	*Post not Sanctioned*	*Teaching Sports Furniture Facilities are Nil/ Inadequate*	*Appointment of Teachers are not on Merit*	*Government Authorities are Biased/ Arrogant*
1.	Andhra Pradesh	-	-	-	-
2.	Bihar	Yes	Yes	Yes	Yes
3.	Chandigarh	-	-	-	Yes
4.	Delhi	-	-	Yes	-
5.	Gujarat	-	-	-	-
6.	Karnataka	-	-	-	Yes
7.	Kerala	-	Yes	-	Yes
8.	Maharashtra	Yes	-	-	Yes
9.	Orissa	-	Yes	-	-
10.	Punjab	-	-	Yes	-
11.	Tamil Nadu	Yes	-	Yes	-
12.	Uttar Pradesh	Yes	Yes	-	-

APPENDIX VII
GRIEVANCES IN MMEI

Sl. No.	State/U.T.	Delay in Recognition	Rejection of Proposals for Institution (professional/technical)	Permission and Recognition of New Classes is Denied/ Delayed	Complicated Procedures Unnecessary Paperwork
1.	Andhra Pradesh	Yes	Yes	Yes	Yes
2.	Bihar	-	-	-	Yes
3.	Chandigarh	-	-	-	-
4.	Delhi	Yes	-	-	-
5.	Gujarat	-	-	-	-
6.	Karnataka	-	-	-	-
7.	Kerala	Yes	-	-	Yes
8.	Maharashtra	-	-	-	-
9.	Orissa	-	-	-	-
10.	Punjab	-	-	-	-
11.	Tamil Nadu	Yes	-	-	Yes
12.	Uttar Pradesh	Yes	Yes	Yes	-

APPENDIX VIII
GRIEVANCES IN MMEI

Sl. No.	State/U.T.	Untrained Teachers due to Lack of Qualified Persons	Delay in Renewal of Recognition Staff Salary	Delay in According Minority Status	Delay in Teaching and Non-teaching	Non-salary Grants Formula is Deficient	Sanction of Leave is Delayed
1.	Andhra Pradesh	Yes	Yes	Yes	Yes	Yes	Yes
2.	Bihar	-	-	-	Yes	-	-
3.	Chandigarh	-	-	-	Yes	-	-
4.	Delhi	Yes	-	-	-	-	-
5.	Gujarat	-	-	-	-	-	-
6.	Karnataka	-	-	-	-	Yes	-
7.	Kerala	-	-	-	-	-	-
8.	Maharashtra	Yes	-	-	-	Yes	-
9.	Orissa	-	-	-	-	-	-
10.	Punjab	-	-	-	Yes	-	Yes
11.	Tamil Nadu	-	-	-	Yes	-	Yes
12.	Uttar Pradesh	-	-	Yes	Yes	-	Yes

APPENDIX IX

High Power Panel on Minorities, Scheduled Castes, Scheduled Tribes and other weaker sections constituted by the Ministry of Home Affairs, Government of India, conducted a survey in 45 districts in 12 States and published their reports almost fifteen years ago (1983), about the minorities. Some of their findings which are put in Appendix form here are very significant to understand the critical problem of the education of the minorities.

SURVEY REPORT OF HIGH POWER PANEL ON MINORITIES ON ENROLMENT

(A) (I) AT ELEMENTARY SCHOOL STAGE (CLASS I TO VIII)

Religious Minority Group	*Enrolment*	*Percentage*	*Corresponding Population Percentage*	*Coverage*
Muslims	12.3	Lower	17.3	12 states 45 districts
Christians	3.7	Higher	2.3	12 states 32 districts
Sikhs	5.8	Higher	4.0	10 states 24 districts
Buddhists	2.2	Lower	6.2	1 state 4 districts

(II) AT SECONDARY SCHOOL STAGE (IX TO XII)

Religious Minority Group	*Enrolment*	*Percentage*	*Corresponding Population Percentage*	*Coverage*
Muslims	10.6	Lower	18.5	11 states 38 districts
Christians	2.2	Higher	0.9	34 districts
Sikhs	3.5	Lower	4.1	10 states 24 districts
Buddhists	1.7	Lower	6.2	1 state 4 districts

APPENDIX IX
AN ANALYSIS OF EXAMINATION RESULTS

AT CLASS X LEVEL

Religious Minority Group	*Percentage of Students who Appeared in Examination*	*Corres-ponding Popula-tion*	*Pass Percentage*	*(Average) General Pass Percentage*	*Coverage*
Muslims	4.0 (Lower)	11.2	59.0 (Higher)	54.0	8 Boards of Secondary Education
Christians	0.8 (Higher)	0.6	60.0 (Higher)	53.9	5 Boards of Secondary Education
Sikhs	14.8 (Higher)	7.7	53.4 (Lower)	51.7	4 Boards of Secondary Education
Buddhists	1.2 (Lower)	6.4	40.6 (Lower)	51.2	2 Boards of Secondary Education
Parsis	0.23 (Higher)	0.14	66.5 (Higher)	51.2	1 Board of Secondary Education
			CLASS XII LEVEL		
Muslims	2.4 (Lower)	10.3	59.7 (Low)	60.8	5 Boards of Higher Secondary
Christians	0.19 (Lower)	1.02	61.14 (High)	60.7	4 Boards of Higher Secondary
Sikhs	10.82 (Low)	22.13	52.02 (Low)	56.52	3 Boards of Higher Secondary
			AT GRADUATE LEVEL (B.A., B.Sc., B.Com.)		
Muslims	6.21 (Low)	10.73	61.3 (Low)	77.1	21 Univer-sities
Christians	3.72 (High)	2.50	63.7 (Low)	60.0	13 Univer-sities
Sikhs	8.85 (High)	3.29	47.76 (Low)	53.66	10 Univer-sities

AT POSTGRADUATE LEVEL (M.A., M.Sc., M.Com.)

Muslims	9.11 (Low)	10.95	75.85 (Low)	77.59	16 Universities
Christians	4.62 (High)	2.92	70.77 (Low)	79.94	9 Universities
Sikhs	8.90 (High)	3.29	56.22 (Low)	78.42	9 Universities

PROFESSIONAL DEGREE COURSES

Muslims B.Sc. (Engg.)	3.41 (Low)	12.44	45 (Low)	65.00	9 Universities
M.B.B.S.	3.44 (Low)	9.55	52.04 (Low)	62.71	12 Universities
Christians					
B.Sc. (Eng.)/BE	7.23 (High)	5.40	80.65 (Low)	90.64	5 Universities
M.B.B.S.	6.14 (High)	4.02	75.72 (Low)	78.27	6 Universities
Sikhs					
B.Sc. (Eng.)/BE	1.70	-	88.10 (High)	82.21	4 Universities
M.B.B.S.	7.42	-	61.11 (High)	52.61	4 Universities
Buddhists					
B.Sc. (Eng.)/BE	1.20	-	60.0 (Low)	71.30	1 University
M.B.B.S.	0.85	-	83.33 (Low)	94.92	1 University
Parsis					
B.Sc. (Eng.)/BE	0.24	-	100.00 (High)	-	1 University
M.B.B.S.	0.56	-	50.00 (Low)	94.92	1 University

Selected Bibliography

Books and Public Documents

Andhra Pradesh, Minorities Commission approach paper on challenge in education vis-a-vis minorities in Andhra Pradesh, Resolution of the A.P. Minorities Commission, Hyderabad: Govt. Central Press, 1980, p. 31.

Arun Kumar, 1985, *Cultural and Educational Rights of the Minorities under Indian Constitution*, New Delhi: Deep and Deep Publications.

Bal, A.K.S., 1976, Anatomy of Minorities Psychology in Jabalpur City, Filed Project Report, New Delhi: I.I.P.A., p. v.

Catholic Bishops Conference of India, C.B.C.I. Centre, 1980, Judgements on minority educational right, 2nd ed., New Delhi: Catholic Bishops Conference of India, p. 444.

Chaklader, Snehamoy, 1981, *Linguistic Minority as a Cohesive force in Indian Federal Process*, New Delhi: Associated, p. 129.

Election Manifesto 1998 (Bhartiya Janata Party).

Ethnic, Groups, 1990, Minorities and Race in Plural Societies in Giddens, Anthony, *Sociology*, Cambridge: Polity Press, pp. 243-46.

Ghurye, G.S., 1974, *Whither India?* Bombay: Popular Prakashan.

Hardy, Peter, 1972, *The Muslims of British India*, Cambridge University Press.

Henry, K. Junekerstroff, 1961, *World Minorities*, Calcutta: Bookland.

Hunter, W.W., 1872, *The Indian Mussalmans*, (2nd edition), London: Trubner & Co.

Hussain, S., Abid, 1965, *The Destiny of Indian Muslims*, Bombay: Asia Publishing House.

India, Committee for Review of National Policy on Education, 1986, Final Report, New Delhi, Department of Education, 1990, p. 409.

India, Department of Education, National Policy on Education, 1986: Implementation Report, New Delhi: The Department of Education, 1988, p. 70.

India, Education Commission, 1882, Report 1883, p. 639, (President Hunter, W.W).

India, High Power Panel on Minorities, SCs/STs & other Weaker Sections, Report on Minorities, New Delhi, 1983.

India, Lok Sabha Secretariat, National Education Policy, New Delhi, The Secretariat, 1985, p. 41.

India, Ministry of Education, Challenge of Education: A Policy Perspective, New Delhi, Ministry of Education, 1985, p. 119.

India, Ministry of Education, National Policy on Education, 1968, p. 10.

India, Ministry of Human Resource Development, Department of Education, *Annual Report*, New Delhi: The Ministry, 1989-90.

India, Ministry of Human Resource Development, Department of Education, Educational Institutions and Judicial Control Analysis and Guidelines, New Delhi, 1987.

India, Minorities Commission, 1971, Report, Delhi: Controller of Publication, 1971.

India, Minorities Commission, Eight Annual Report of the Minorities Commission for the period 1.4.85 to 31.3.86, Delhi, Controller of Publications.

Judgements of Minority Educational Rights, Catholic Bishops' Conference of India, New Delhi, C.B.C.I. Centre, 1980 (2nd Ed.).

Kerala, Commission for Reservation of Seats in Educational Institutions, 1964, Report 1965, p. 142, (Chairman: Sh. G. Kumara Pillai).

Kerala, High Level Committee on Education and Employment, 1982. Report, Trivandrum, State Planning Board, 1984, p. v.

Krishna, K.B., 1939, *The Problem of Minorities in India*, London: George Allen & Unwin Ltd.

Laponce, J.A., 1960, *The Protection of Minorities*, University of California Press.

Louis, Wirth, 1965, 'The Problem of Minorities Group' in Talcott Parsons et.al. (eds.), *The Theories of Society*.

Mujeeb, M., 1967, *The Indian Muslims*, London: George Allen & Unwin.

Muse and the Minorities Social Congress and Creative Cohesion, Saket, New Delhi, 1998.

Nehru, Jawaharlal, 1946, *The Discovery of India*, Calcutta, Signet Press.

Orissa, Directorate of Public Institution. Report on the fourth educational Survey, Orissa, 1982, Bhubaneshwar, The Directorate, 1982, p. 231.

Panikkar, K.M., 1963, *The Foundations of the New India*, London: George Allen & Unwin.

Rights of religious minorities to establish and administer educational institutions. In Kashyap, Anirban, *Disintegration and Constitution*, pp. 117-93 New Delhi, Lancers, 1990.

Rose, A.M. & Rose, C.B. (eds.), 1965, *Minority Problem*, New York: Harper.

Seervai, H.M., 1983, *Constitutional Law of India*, pp. 937-78, Third Edition, Vol. I, Bombay, N.M. Tripathy.

Sen, D., 1940, *The Problem of Minorities*, University of Calcutta.

Shah, A.K., *Educational and Educational Institutions Cases* (1950-91).

Shah, S., Shamim, Educational survey report on Muslim-managed schools and colleges in India, With special emphasis on science education, New Delhi, Hamdard, Education Society, 1982-83, p. 226.

Shaigir, M., 1980, *Politics of Minorities: Some Perspectives*, p. 172, Delhi, Ajanta.

Shakir, M., 1989, *Religion State and Politics in India*, pp. 155-199, 249-270, Delhi: Ajanta.

Sharma, G.S., 1973, *Educational and Cultural Rights of the Minorities: A Study in Social Effects of the Judicial Trends in India*, p. 51, New Delhi, Indian Council of Social Sciences Research.

Sharma, K.D., 1978, *Education of a National Minority*, New Delhi, Kalamkar.

Thakur, R.N., 1998, Concept of Minority and Consociational Model in a Plural Society in *Dimension of Federal Nation Building*, (ed.), by Abdul Rahim, P.Vijapur Centre for Federal Studies, New Delhi, Jamia Hamdard and Manak Publications.

Thakur, R.N., Report of the Research Study of the Grievances relating to the Minority Managed Educational Institutions Functioning under various State/U.T. Administrations in India, Vols. I-III. Indian Institute of Public Administration, New Delhi and Minorities Commission, Government of India, 1992-93.

Uttar Pradesh, Bhasha Vibhag, Facilities provided for linguistic minorities in Uttar Pradesh, pp. 41, 196.

Uttar Pradesh, Minorities Commission Annual Report, p. 316, Lucknow, 1975.

Wadhwa, Kamlesh Kumar, 1975, *Minority Safeguards in India (Constitutional Provisions and their Implementation)*, p. 273, Delhi, Thompson.

Weiner, Myron, 1986, India's Minorities: Who Are They?' In James, R. Roach (ed.), *India 2000: the next fifteen years*, Maryland (USA): The Riverdale Co.

Wilson, Anil, 1992, 'Minority institutions: not a merited judgement', *The Hindustan Times* (19 June).

Wirth Loris, 'The Problem of Minority Groups' in Talcott Parsons et al. (eds.) *Theories of Society*, pp. 309-15, New York: The Free Press.

Yaqin, Anwarul, 1982, *Constitutional Protection of Minority Educational Institutions in India*, New Delhi, Deep & Deep Publications.

Articles (Periodicals and Newspapers)

Ahmad Imtiaz, Muslim Educational Backwardness: An Inferential Analysis, *Economic & Political Weekly*, 16(36): 1457-65.

Ahmad Imtiaz, Promoting Education among Muslims, *The Times of India* (8 Aug; 1988).

Ahmad, Faian, Minorities Panel gets Legal Status, *Telegraph* (5 Aug; 1991).

Ansari, Iqbal, A Fresh Look at Minority Right, *Free Press Journal* (28 June, 1990).

Bakshi, P.M., Labour Law and Minorities, *Financial Express* (25 June; 1988).

Bakshi, P.M., Law and Minority Institutions, *Financial Express* (12 March; 1988).

Banerjee, Shashwata, Minority Complex: The Malady of all Indians, *Statesman* (6 August; 1991).

Black Bill Triggers row in Bihar, *Hindu* (28 August; 1991).

Chadha, G.S., Crusade against Injustice, *Spokesman* (7 Nov., 1988) 8:1

Devadason, E.D., Meaning and Implications of Minority Rights, *New Frontiers in Education*, 12:2 (April-June, 1982) 25-9.

Devadason, E.D., Rights of Minority Institutions. *Hindu* (7 April, 1992) 17.

Development Panel for Minorities Urged, *Patriot* (15 Sep., 1991).

Engineer, Asghar Ali, Muslim Minority in India and Hindu Minority in Pakistan: A Comparative Review, *Mainstream*, 29(21) 16 Mar. 1991, 11-12 14.

Engineer, Asghar Ali, Minorities and Poll: A Comparison, *Hindu* (14 Apr., 1992) 8.

———, Fair Deal to Minorities, *Yojana* (1 July, 1988) 22-24.

Fifteen-point Plan for Minorities to be Recast, *Indian Express* (31 March, 1992).

The Forgotten Report of Gopal Singh's Panel on Minorities, *Muslim India*, 2:22 (8 October, 1984), 465-7, 2:23 (November, 1984) 52-5; 2:24 (December 1984) 571-4.

Gill, S.S., Tilting at Windmills, *Illustrated Weekly of India*, 101(4), 26 Jan., 1991, 34-5.

Gupta, Bishan Swarup, Equality of Educational Opportunity and Muslims: A comparative study of rural schools of four districts in U.P. with reference to schools culture, textbooks and facilities for teaching Urdu and through Urdu, *Indian Educational Review*, 18:2 (April, 1983) 84-91.

Gupta, O.P., Why Muslim Community, Shuns Government Schools in U.P., *Muslim India*, 1:11 (November, 1983), 508-10.

Jayaram, N., Ethnicity and Education: A Socio-Historical Perspective on the Educational Backwardness of Indian Muslims, *Sociological Bulletin*, Vol. 39, Nos. 1 & 2, 1990, pp. 115-30.

Jha, Nambiar, Sanora, St. Stephen's Case: Minority Institutions may Seek Review, *The Times of India* (6 April, 1992).

Judgement in St. Stephen's Case called Flawed, *The Times of India* (31 March, 1992).

Kapur, N.S., Educational Rights of Minorities, *The Hindustan Times*, (3 Jan., 1992).

Minority Institutions, *Patriot* (20 December, 1991).

Minorities Panel Conducting Study, *Deccan Herald* (25.2.1992).

Minorities should merge in common Indian identity, *Organiser*, 36:44 (17 March 1985) 6.

Minority Commission, Lok Sabha, *USQ* No. 106. (15 July, 1991).

Rajya Sabha, *USQ* No. 143. (16 July 1991).

Muslim Education in India: An Educational Survey, *Educational Review*, 90:7-8 (July-August, 1984) 122.

Muslim Education in India, *Educational Review*, 94:8 (August 1988), 140.

National Agenda for Governance (19 March, 1998, *The Economic Times*)

Noorani, A.G., Minorities Commission: A Year's Performance, *Indian Express*, (22 March, 1979).

Noorani, A.G., Minorityism and Minorities, *Indian Express* (6 July, 1991).

A note on Minority Institutions, *New Quest* 32 (March-April 1982), 101-4.

Panel for Welfare of Minorities, L.S. *USQ* No. 7051 (2 May 90).

Prabhu, Louella Lobo, Tokenism and the Minorities, *Insight* (22 July, 1988), 3,7.

Razdan, Deepak, Minorities Panel Submits Report, *The Hindustan Times*, (14 July, 1991).

A Rejoinder to Sadhaba's article: Our Instable Minorities, *Sarvodaya*, 32, 1-2, (July-August, 1985) 19-20.

Row Over Minority College Laws, *The Hindu* (23 October, 1992).

Roy, Bhaskar, Indian Muslims: At a Turning-point, *Indian Express* (22 Sep., 1991).

Supreme Court Judgement on Minority Institutions, *The Times of India*, (7 December, 1991).

Sahay, S., A Debatable Judgement, *The Hindustan Times* (13 December, 1991); *The Times of India* (13 December, 1991).

Sadhana, Our Insatiable Minorities, *Sarvodaya*, 32: 11-12 (May-June, 1985) 498-500.

Sathe, S.P., Minorities and the Law, *Pariance*, 8:2-3 (November-December, 1984), 25-9.

Scheme for the Welfare of Minorities, L.S. *USQ* No. 6271 (9 September, 1991).

Shahabuddin, Syed, Muslim Education in India: Self-identity and National Purpose, *Islam and Modern Age*, 15:1 (February 1984). 61-8.

Singh, Kanwaldeep, MP Tribal Schools on the Threshold of Closure, *Indian Express* (29 July, 1991).

Singh, Parmanand, Academic and Administrative Freedom of Minority Institutions in India, *Journal of the Indian Law Institute*, 19(3), July-Sep., 77, 296-312.

Srinivasan, Nirmala, Minorities Commission—A Critique, *Indian Express*, 31 Jan., 1978, p. 6.

Statutory Status Bill for Minorities Panel, *The Hindustan Times*, (31 March, 1992).

Thampu, Valson, Minority Colleges: Key SC Verdict, *The Times of India*, (1 April, 1992).

Thampu, Valson, Minority Institutions: Principle of Merit and SC Verdict, *The Hindustan Times* (24 April, 1992).

Trivedy, Shikha, Minorities Commission: A Major Issue, *Economic Times*, (10 June, 1991).

Viswanathan, Aparna, Federalism will not Protect Minorities, *The Times of India* (10 January, 1992).

Vivek, Hindu Bomb: Castes and Minorities, *Frontier* (20 Aug., 1988) 4-8.

Welfare of Minorities under 15 Points Programme, Lok Sabha *USQ*. No. 740 (9 Sep., 1991).

Index